Zimmermann
& Zimmermann

Maths, Stress + a Lovesick Heart

Aus dem Deutschen
von Anne Dettmer

Thienemann

The day

began well enough. In the morning I found my long-lost glove in my history book, so my hands were nice and warm again on the way to school, even though it was bitterly cold. And then we got our maths test back – absolutely **spot on**! On the way home from school my friend Tanja and I managed to grab the last two seats on the tram. We **winked** at each other. Let the others have a taste of being **squashed up** like sardines.

But I had my best joker up my sleeve, or rather in my school bag. I really felt like grinning, but Tanja was staring at me with such a worried look that I tried to look as sorrowful as possible.

"I know it must be awful for you," started my best friend, leaning over towards me. "How are you going to tell your parents?"

I shrugged my shoulders. "Don't know. I'll wait and see."

---

spot on – Volltreffer; to wink – zuzwinkern;
to squash up – zusammenrücken

Tanja's face flushed. She really was very concerned about me. "Perhaps I could have helped you," she said, "honestly, I really do blame myself that …"

"It's alright, Tanja, really, I know," I interrupted her, "but it's not your fault if, in the first place, I don't **bother** learning anything, and then I get a complete blackout in middle of the test."

Poor Tanja was quite **bewildered**. But I suppose it is a bit confusing when your best friend, who has had an **A** in maths ever since you can remember, ends up with a D to E, all of a sudden. And then you yourself – normally scrabbling around at the bottom third of the class – suddenly discover a B minus in your workbook. Tanja could not show any joy about her good grade in front of me. She was probably glad to get off the tram three stops before me. But then again, that's exactly how I felt. I waved **fleetingly** and nodded when she shouted to say she would be phoning me that very afternoon. I then sat back with a sense of satisfaction. Everything had worked out splendidly, and the rest would be child's play. I looked out of the window and felt how my heart started **pounding**. There was the number 13 approaching on the neighbouring **track**, the very tram where everything started. A day I would remember in a hundred years to come.

---

to bother – sich die Mühe machen, etwas zu tun;
bewildered – verblüfft; A – Note Eins; fleetingly – flüchtig;
to pound – hämmern, klopfen; track – Gleis

It was a cold and foggy November morning, and it was **drizzling**.

"Weather for colds," remarked Dad at breakfast, and sneezed three times, just to prove his point.

Mum didn't even glance up from her newspaper. "That's something we can **do without** at the moment," she simply said and scribbled something on the **margin** of the newspaper. "There's an awful lot to be done at work," she continued.

My parents both work at the same computer company, and, as always in the run up to Christmas, all **hell is let loose**. "People buy their kids the most expensive computers, and are then surprised when their little darlings manage to break them **in next to no time**," moaned Dad. "And then we have to listen to all the complaints. Anyway, I think computers are ..."

"Do be quiet, please," my mother interrupted him, "that sort of talk is bad for business."

Dad winked at me and sneezed for the fourth time.

Mum gave him a **withering** look. "I just told you that we can't afford to catch a cold at the moment."

"Did you hear that? I'm not even allowed to be ill," Dad complained to me. "I really do envy you. A nice morning in school, legs stretched out under the table, and the teachers doing their very best at the

---

to drizzle – nieseln; to do without – verzichten; margin – Seitenrand; hell is let loose – der Teufel ist los; in next to no time – in null Komma nix; withering – vernichtend

front trying to keep **you lot** entertained. Oh, to be young again." He sighed **wistfully** and opened up his laptop.

The joys of youth? You've got to be kidding! **Dreary** and boring! That's what my life was like. Well, on days like this at least. What do you expect on a grey November morning, when you've got cold feet and a full timetable with double German, English, Maths, Music and Biology on top of all that? Nothing. Absolutely nothing. At least, that's what I thought. But fate **had** something else **in mind** for me.

The "cold weather" also seemed to have spread around our school teachers. At any rate, three of them were **off sick** all at once, and so Tanja and I were out of school after the third lesson. The stupid thing was that we missed the tram by seconds, and so we stood around in the cold, quite annoyed. I would have preferred to have gone to the café at the market square. Tanja, too, but she just couldn't afford it. Since her parents had got divorced, her pocket money was rather **meagre**. I could have invited to pay for her coke, of course, but that would have seemed like **bragging**. Anyway, I was saving up for a new pair of **trainers**. So what were we supposed to do – stand around a solid half hour waiting for the next num-

---

you lot – euch alle; wistfully – wehmütig; dreary – öde; to have sth in mind – etwas vorhaben; to be off sick – wegen Krankheit fehlen; meagre – mager; to brag – angeben, prahlen; trainers – Turnschuhe

ber 16 to come? Even a lesson of biology would have been better than that.

"Hey look, there comes the number 13. It doesn't really go in our direction, but **what the heck**? Shall we?"

Tanja and I looked at each other. Every now and again we have our mad ideas. We decided to spend a **leisurely** morning, riding around in the tram with our monthly travel pass.

The tram was wonderfully empty and, above all, warm. We made ourselves comfortable, shared a **currant bun** and had a good gossip. "Guess what, Marko asked me if I wanted to join the school choir." Tanja put her hand in front of her mouth so as not to spit out her currant bun for laughing.

"Well?" I asked with interest. "Are you going to?"

"Are you joking?" Tanja got cross. "Marko asks everybody! And anyway, you'll never catch me singing in the school choir. You have to go singing Christmas carols in old people's homes and all that stuff. Anyway, Marko isn't my type."

She stared longingly into the distance while she **bored** around in her piece of currant bun. "There was a brilliant thriller on telly last night. With a new detective. He was **gorgeous**. Tall, shoulder-length blond curls, blue eyes. What a dream." She sighed in a low voice. "The stupid thing is that I missed

---

what the heck – was soll's; leisurely – gemütlich;
currant bun – Rosinenbrötchen; to bore – bohren;
gorgeous – atemberaubend

the credits. Do you think I should ring up the television station to find out who he is, and where he lives?"

I nodded. Tanja asks me the same question at least once a month. For years now, she's been **raving about** some actor that nobody has ever heard of. She'll probably be dreaming of some star or other when she's an old age pensioner.

I had dreams of my own, of course. One in particular at the time was the promotion of my girls' football team into the regional league. We might even get sponsored, and be able to buy a club bus. We ought to have an extra day of training, I reflected, as we're pretty weak in attack. Perhaps we could put Marelina on the left-wing, and then I would have …

"You're not listening to me at all," complained Tanja, **straightening** her glasses.

"I am, I am," I answered, feeling guilty, and put on an interested face when she started to **relate** the whole story involving the inspector who had made such an impression on her.

"He's got the most incredible eyes. I hope someone in our class had their video recorder on. I might have another chance then. **Blast**! Look there, in front of you. He must be absolutely crazy." She stood up excitedly.

---

the credits – Abspann eines Films; to rave about – schwärmen für; to straighten – zurechtrücken; to relate – nacherzählen; blast! – Mist!

There was an old R4 standing at the **junction** in front, and the driver was trying to re-start the engine but not with much luck.

"And over there, the people, just look how they're **gawping**!" Tanja pointed to the track next to us where the tram was just stopping, and grimaced.

I was pretty embarrassed; hopefully no-one was looking towards us. Tanja really can get on your nerves at times. I **peeked** through the window pane that was very dirty indeed. I could faintly see my own reflection. There were only a few people in the other tram. Most of the passengers had gone to the back, curious to watch the driver who had by this time got out, and was trying to push the car from the junction. Only one of the passengers was not taking the slightest bit of interest in what was happening outside. A boy with dark brown curls who seemed to be so **engrossed** in his book that he didn't notice anything around him. What could he be reading, I wondered.

Just at that moment he looked up. Our eyes met. It was fortunate that I was sitting down, as I felt **dizzy**. I sensed how my heart was beating loudly, and for a moment I was feeling incredibly **blissful**. That's what they call love at first sight, it flashed through my mind.

"Henri, are you alright? What's the matter?"

---

junction – Kreuzung; to gawp – gaffen; to peek – gucken; engrossed – vertieft; dizzy – schwindlig, schummerig; blissful – glückselig

I swallowed. "Tanja, look over there **inconspicuously**. Look at him, the one with the dark brown curly hair. Do you happen to know him?"

Tanja straightened her glasses. Just at that moment the tram started to move off. Tanja shook her head. "No, I don't think so. Was it important?"

My voice **quavered** as I said: "No, not really. I think I've mistaken him for someone else."

Tanja didn't seem to notice that I was **fibbing**. She was still talking about her film hero, thinking of a new idea of how she might get to know the actor. I nodded at regular intervals. How stupid, I didn't even know the number of the tram in which the boy had been sitting. Otherwise I might have been able to **coincidentally** travel on the same tram. Three times every afternoon, if necessary. I would have met him then sooner or later …

"You're absolutely hopeless," said Tanja, interrupting my delightful fantasies, "I think you're coming down with something. I'm going to get off the next stop and visit my father. He still owes me three months' pocket money, and my horoscope for today says I'm in for a pleasant surprise. Who knows what nice things are waiting for me." She grinned, grabbed her rucksack and waved to me.

At last I could return to my fantasies in peace. I would be sitting there in the tram, and brown curls

---

inconspicuously – unauffällig; to quaver – zittern, beben; to fib – schwindeln; coincidentally – zufällig

would get on. He would sit down next to me, of course. And what then? Should I just speak to him? If only I could be more **daring**. Like Tanja, for example. For her it's no problem at all reciting a poem in front of the whole school. And I get into a panic even if I have to read out my homework in class. In my imagination I could see how the boy would sit next to me for a few stops and then get off the tram. I shook my head resolutely. I just had to overcome my **shyness**. Maybe I could talk to him about the football league? I knew all about football. In any event, it wouldn't be easy just talking to a complete stranger, especially one I **fancied**. I put off these disturbing thoughts for the time being, and put my mind to working out the best training programme for my team.

By the time I got home, I'd almost forgotten brown curls, and in the afternoon I had quite other problems to worry about during football training. Our **goalie** was ill, and Maike, who could have taken her place if necessary, couldn't stop sneezing either. **In a nutshell**, it was a complete disaster, yet again. And all that just before qualification for the regional league!

"You and your ambition," grumbled my mother when I let off my frustration at supper. "Other girls of your age learn to ride or do ballet. Where on earth did you get all this football **mania** from?"

---

daring – mutig; shyness – Schüchternheit;
to fancy sb – auf jmd. stehen; goalie – Torhüter;
in a nutshell – kurz gesagt; mania – Fimmel, Besessenheit

She gave Dad a questioning look. He **started** slightly. "Well, it's not so terrible if just one of three daughters happens to take a bit of interest in football ..." He didn't get any further than that because he had to sneeze. "Coming down with a cold," he mumbled. "I'm off to bed so I'll be top fit again tomorrow."

"I'm going to bed," I said. "I've had a stressful day, too."

That was a **gross** exaggeration, of course, but I didn't feel like explaining to my mother for the thousandth time exactly why and how I came to play in a girls' football team, and why I didn't want to play a dying swan in ballet. No thank you! I went to my sister Babette's room and fetched her CD player with headphones, and at the same time borrowed two of her new CD's. They were still packed in cellophane so I had to open them, unfortunately. Normally, I would have asked Babette, but as she was away in Freiburg studying maths, I couldn't very well get in touch with her all that quickly. I would beg her forgiveness at the weekend for listening to the new CD's before her.

I sat on the window sill, put in the first CD and stared outside into the darkness. Ten minutes later I was already crying my eyes out. I hadn't noticed the kind of music my sister **inflicts upon herself**. French

---

to start – zusammenzucken; gross – grob;
to inflict sth upon oneself – sich etwas antun

chansons! L'amour and all that stuff. Of course, I immediately thought about the boy on the tram, the cute one with the curly hair. The music was entirely unsuitable for those unlucky in love, such as me.

I took a hard rock CD from my eldest sister Anette, and turned it up full volume. By the third track, when my ears were nearly falling off and I had regained my former optimism, someone suddenly tore the headphones from my head. Dad, in his pyjamas with a thick woollen scarf wrapped around his neck, was holding out the telephone receiver to me.

"Henriette, are you deaf?" he ranted. "The phone has been ringing for ten minutes. Mum is sitting in front of the computer and doesn't feel **responsible**. And neither do you, eh? And poor, sick me has to get out of bed." He put his hand over the mouthpiece. "Kindly inform you friend Tanja that phone calls after ten o'clock at night are regarded as a **physical assault** in this house."

I muttered something like "yeah, yeah." There were two possibilities: either Tanja wanted to know what homework we had to do for tomorrow. Or she wanted to tell me how she could find out the name of that **actor**. That could have waited until tomorrow, I thought, and I was therefore not too friendly when I answered the phone.

---

responsible – zuständig; physical assault – Körperverletzung; actor – Schauspieler

"Henri, I've really got something to tell you," she started. "I was just flicking through the TV guide. You know, because of last night's thriller, the one I was telling you about. And then I remembered our ride on the tram this morning."

"Keep it short," I **snarled**, "I'm dead tired. Or tell me tomorrow." I **yawned** loudly into the receiver.

"Oh, alright then. I just thought you'd be interested to know who that boy on the tram was. You see, it just **occurred** to me ..."

"Sorry? What did you say?" I interrupted her, and suddenly my voice didn't sound very tired any more. "You mean the one with the brown curly hair? Go on, tell me!"

"Yep, that's the one. But of course, if you're too tired to talk on the phone, we could talk about it in school tomorrow."

"Oh **rubbish**, Tanja, I'm **wide awake** now. We can talk all night long as far as I'm concerned. Go on, tell me what occurred to you."

Tanja laughed. "Chat all night long? Can you imagine how my mother would moan about the telephone bill. No, what I wanted to tell you: I now know who the boy is. You won't believe it, but ..." she paused for a short while, and I noticed how I held my breath out of sheer excitement.

"He's Doctor Caberg's son," she continued.

---

to snarl – knurren; to yawn – gähnen;
to occur – hier: einfallen; rubbish – Quatsch;
wide awake – hellwach

That really took my breath away. "Honestly? Caberg's son?" I asked in surprise.

"Exactly, Mrs Caberg, our math's teacher. Her son's name is Tom. I know that because my divorced dad's girlfriend lives in the same house as Caberg. Anyway, I **bumped into him**, and I heard Caberg call him Tom."

Tanja. My very best of friends. Rings up selflessly late at night, risks a **ticking off** from my father, and all that just to tell me that the boy with the brown curly hair is called Tom Caberg. I could have **hugged** her.

"Tomorrow I'll help you find out the name of that actor who played the detective," I promised.

That night I slept exceptionally well, as I felt I had made quite a bit of progress. I'd fallen in love at lunchtime, and twelve hours later I already knew his name. That was **considerable** progress, I thought. If only things would keep going at this pace! Even Babette had found herself a boyfriend lately, and the only subject Babette can talk about is higher mathematics.

That night I dreamed about our **battle for promotion** into the regional league, and all the players on the opposing team were teddy bears, all with brown curls.

---

to bump into sb – hier: jmd. zufällig begegnen; ticking off – Anschiss; to hug – umarmen; considerable – beachtlich; battle for promotion – Aufstiegskampf

"Hey, you there, are you dreaming?" The voice of the conductor on the tram sounded **concerned**. "We arrived at the **terminus** ten minutes ago, and you're still sitting here."

I got up hastily, grabbed my school bag and muttered something incomprehensible. I really had been so deep in thought that I even forgot to get off the tram. And I had every reason to hurry up as I absolutely wanted to have lunch together with my parents. I grinned and tapped three times on my school bag. I was certain that the plan I'd worked out would not fail. After all, I had known my parents and their weaknesses long enough.

"I'm only doing it all **for the sake of** Tom," I reassured myself when my guilty **conscience** started to **prick** me for not being entirely honest.

Ten yards in front of the house I put on my bad-tempered face. I kept ringing the bell, **barged in** through the door, threw my things in the nearest corner and sat down at the dining table without saying a word. But nobody took any notice of my behaviour. My mother was on the phone and Dad was sitting in the living room with Babette, discussing mathematical problems. What was my sister doing here at home in the middle of the week? She usually only came home at the weekend.

---

concerned – besorgt; terminus – Endstation;
for the sake of sb – jmd. zuliebe; to prick sb conscience – Gewissensbisse bereiten; to barge in – reinplatzen

She had thoroughly messed up my plans, but I just still had to try.

"**It's a good job** we still had something in the freezer," said my mother when we were all sitting at the table. "Babette, here's a chance to **eat your fill** again". She piled a huge portion of lasagne onto her half-starved daughter's plate. "How about you, Henriette? Lasagne is one of your favourite meals!"

You could hear my stomach rumbling, but I remained steadfast. "No thanks, I've got no appetite today," I said in a pathetic voice. The lasagne looked incredibly delicious but I had to **turn it down**.

Unfortunately, nobody asked me why I didn't want to eat anything. Babette was talking about her **thesis**, and mum was moaning about the computer problems expected for the year 2000. Dad shovelled in a second portion of lasagne, without saying a word.

"By the way, I got my maths test back today," I said at last when Babette stopped to take a short breath before dessert.

"Oh yes?" said mum. "Would you go and get the vanilla custard and chocolate sauce out of the fridge, dear?"

"… Well, unfortunately, the maths test …"

"Henri, will you go and get the dessert at last. I'm being picked up at four, and I want to talk a few

---

it's a good job – wie gut, dass …; to eat one's fill – sich satt essen; to turn sth down – etwas ablehnen; thesis – Diplomarbeit things through with our parents," Babette interrupted me.

I went into the kitchen and hated my family for a whole five minutes, during which I stuffed myself with four **helpings** of vanilla custard and chocolate sauce. I wasn't hungry any more after that, at any rate. But unfortunately, I was also feeling pretty sick. If they had let me finish talking at lunch, I would also have had some of the lasagne, I thought as I went into the dining room to say that there wasn't any dessert.

Mum looked astonished, and Dad was **outraged**, exclaiming that he'd put the dessert bowls in the fridge himself. Had I gone blind, he wanted to know. But I simply ignored them and went to my room to **have a think**. I had a plan and a definite target. I simply had to get to know Tom Caberg, now that I'd been dreaming about him at least every second night for about two weeks. And I didn't mean "get to know" in the sense of bumping into him on the tram and just saying hello, oh no, I meant *really* "get to know." I was prepared to make a few **sacrifices** for this. And that was exactly what I was doing since Tanja had told me that Tom was my maths teacher's son.

Actually my plan was as simple as it was brilliant, and was based on experience gained during early childhood – the most **formative** years in a child's life. That's what I'd read in a parent's guide that my

---

helping – Portion; outraged – empört; to have a think – gründlich nachdenken; sacrifice – Opfer; formative – prägend

mother had left lying around on her bedside table. At the age of seven when I was not able to work out fifteen minus eight in a tenth of a second, my parents went into a state of crisis, and wondered whether I was really their daughter or not. Anyway, that's more or less what they said at my grandparents' golden wedding anniversary.

A mathematical mind is in our family genes. It may sound funny to some people, but maths is just great fun for all of us. So when the youngest daughter comes home with bad marks in her favourite subject, the parents feel the family tradition is **at stake**. There is only one thing that can help: extra lessons, preferably with Dr Caberg who, as dear Henrietta's maths teacher, best knows what her weaknesses are. That was my plan. And once I'd started having extra lessons with Caberg, then I was sure to meet Tom. He would then fall in love with me, and a few in my class would be greatly surprised! It was all quite simple, or so I thought.

The only trouble was that nobody seemed to take any interest in my maths marks. It wasn't until late afternoon when Babette was on her way back to Freiburg at last, that I dared make a second attempt.

"I've got to tell you something," I said, and remained standing at the living room door.

Dad looked up **startled**. "Is she **pregnant**?" he asked and looked at Mum inquiringly.

---

to be at stake – in Gefahr sein; startled – erschrocken; pregnant – schwanger

She shook her head in annoyance. "Well really, Rainer, I ask you! Henriette isn't even fourteen yet."

Dad just said that you never knew these days, and he was glad that I wasn't going to turn him into a grandfather just yet.

But the shock I was about to give my parents was also like **dropping a bombshell**. I sat down next to Dad and shoved my exercise book with the poisonous green cover under his nose.

"We got our maths test back, and I got a D to E. The class average was B minus!"

Dad pulled a face. "So what am I supposed to do? Shout hurray? Anke what do you think?"

Mum pulled up a chair with the tip of her toe, and sat down first of all. I think she was pretty shocked. And then she got going: "I've been saying for ages that Henriette has only got silly old football in her head. She has just got to do something for school. It's got nothing to do with her intelligence. It's pure **laziness**."

I'd done an awful lot of revision, I insisted, but lately, I didn't seem to understand all that much. If I had someone to explain it all to me exactly, then …

"Precisely! What is Babette studying maths for? She can surely give her sister **extra tuition** if she can't find a job," said Dad, and glanced longingly towards his daily newspaper. I suspected that he'd

---

to drop a bombshell – eine Bombe platzen lassen; laziness – Faulheit; extra tuition – Nachhilfe

had other ideas for his afternoon at home. "Babette can start right away at the weekend! Problem solved!"

Of course, that's what I was afraid of. Extra tuition with Babette was the worst thing I could possibly imagine. I seriously doubted whether my love for Tom Caberg was strong enough to endure this. But I did have a very good argument against involving the family in my extra tuition.

"Weekends are stupid because Babette wants a bit of peace after all. And you yourselves are always saying that you should leave the rest of the family in peace with professional problems. It only makes living together even more difficult." That made an **impact**. It was one of Dad's phrases, word for word.

He hesitated.

I had to **seize** the opportunity, of course. "I don't want to get even worse in maths, so perhaps I should look for someone to give me extra tuition. I could pay for it out of my savings, or take a part-time job so that I can afford someone who is really good."

My parents looked at me in amazement. I now had to be very careful not to overdo it. "It's only a suggestion," I **toned it down** a little.

Mum laughed. "Yes, let's just wait and see," she suggested. "Henriette is an **ace** at maths and it would

---

impact – Eindruck; to seize – ergreifen;
to tone down – abschwächen; ace – Ass

be a laugh if she didn't get a grade A again in her next test."

Dad looked doubtful. He didn't seem to be quite so sure of his daughter's mathematical abilities. "Perhaps extra tuition would be quite a good thing until she's found her feet again," he suggested, but Mum just **waved him aside**.

"I don't think it will be necessary," she said. "Henriette is just not allowed to go to football training if she doesn't work properly for school. Her **performance** will then improve quite quickly."

For a moment I thought everything had been in vain. I hadn't done a single piece of maths homework for weeks, let alone take an active part in lessons. In the last test, which had been **easy-peasy**, I had forced myself to make silly mistakes. But I did make one important error. I couldn't resist the temptation with the last question. I worked it out correctly. That's why I got only a D to E. If only I'd got a straight F! That would have been a real alarm signal for my parents. But I should have thought of that earlier on.

"We've got quite another problem at the moment," Mum interrupted my thoughts. "Babette has emptied the fridge and taken everything **edible** with her. We haven't got anything left in the house for supper. Henriette, I've made a shopping list. And here's the money. Would you just …?"

---

to wave aside – abwinken; performance – Leistung; easy-peasy – babyleicht; edible – essbar

Half an hour later I was sullenly pushing the trolley around the supermarket. Apart from me, there were about a thousand other people out shopping. The **tills** were busy accordingly. Thinking quickly, I stood behind an older woman who only had a carton of milk in her hand.

At that very moment she turned around and waved the carton of milk around in the air. “Herbert, I’m over here,” she cried, and a white-haired gentleman pushed his way in front of me with a fully-packed trolley. I obviously had to queue up somewhere else. The milk carton had only been a **camouflage**; the couple were probably stocking up for a **famine**.

Undecided, I looked around. It was just as busy everywhere else. I queued up at the next till and stared into my trolley. I knew very well why Mum hadn’t gone shopping herself.

After half an eternity it was my turn at last. I placed the few things that I’d bought onto the **belt**. The cashier was just about to start scanning the goods when a customer came up to her in a nervous state, waving a fifty euro note about in the air.

“You’ve given me a **forged** note,” she cried out in outrage. “The water mark is missing here. I can see it quite clearly!”

Great! The police would probably come along

---

till – Kasse im Supermarkt; camouflage – Tarnung; famine – Hungersnot; belt – Laufband; forged – gefälscht

now, and I would still be standing here the day after tomorrow.

The cashier smiled gently: "Dear Mrs Kilzberg, we know all about it. The police will be here in a minute. Just go and sit down over there until they come."

She **gave me a wink**. "She comes here every day with the same story," she said to me in an undertone, and started scanning the goods.

The customers at the other tills had become alert and were looking across curiously.

A man in a green Loden coat and a Tyrolean hat, who had just finished paying at the till next to me, shouted out loud: "The Mafia are all behind this, as I keep telling my wife."

I **stopped short**. The boy behind him was placing a net of oranges on the belt. Tom! No doubt about it. It was Tom! I would have recognized him on a **pitch-dark** night.

"Thirteen euros and ninety-nine cents," I heard a voice say far off in the distance.

"Haven't you got any money with you? What's the matter?" The cashier looked at me concerned.

All the bystanders were staring at me, curiously. Even Tom had turned around.

For a moment we gazed directly into each other's eyes.

---

to give sb a wink – jmd. zuzwinkern; to stop short – stutzen, aufmerken; pitch-dark – stockfinster

"Are you going to get a move on up there!" someone moaned.

For a moment I searched for my purse in vain until I remembered that I'd put the fifty euro note from Mum into the back pocket of my trousers. I carelessly handed it over to the cashier. Tom had already paid and had turned to go. I now had to **keep up with** him.

"Wait a minute, wait a minute, don't forget your change," the cashier shouted after me and laughed. "Thirty-six euros and one cent. Your mother would have been pleased if you'd forgotten the change." She pressed the money into my hand and mumbled: "The youth of today!"

Right, I had the money, but where was Tom? I searched all around. But **to no avail**. Tom wasn't anywhere to be seen.

I started **mulling** it over. What was Tom doing in this supermarket?

After all, Caberg lives in quite a different part of town. But it then occurred to me that it was Wednesday afternoon, and this was one of the few shops open that afternoon. Caberg had probably forgotten to buy oranges and had driven Tom here especially. While I was still keeping a lookout for him, the both of them were certainly on their way home again.

---

to keep up with sb – mit jmd. Schritt halten; to no avail – vergebens; to mull sth over – über etwas nachdenken

I was frustrated for a moment. But then it occurred to me that, just like in fairy tales, things don't turn out right until the third time. When I see Tom the next time, I thought, then he will fall in love with me, too.

At the moment

everything is working out brilliantly. That's what I thought to myself the next morning on the way to school. Of course, my class mates had noticed in the meantime that their ace at maths had **deteriorated** dramatically. It wasn't a good idea to copy my homework because you could guarantee that everything I'd done was wrong. But apart from Tanja, nobody had said anything to me about it. And Tanja wasn't seriously interested, either. She had quite different problems. She wasn't raving about the detective with the long blond hair any more, but an actor at the local theatre was her latest **heart-throb**. At least she already knew his name, and that was miles of progress in comparison with the previous one. I'll keep it up this week, I swore to myself as I entered the school building. But if it shouldn't work out with Tom at all, then I at least wanted to enjoy maths again.

---

to deteriorate – abbauen, sich verschlechtern;
heart-throb – Schwarm

He doesn't look a bit like his mother, I thought to myself during the maths lesson. He clearly must take after his father, as there was not the slightest **resemblance** between Tom, who was so cute, and Dr Renate Caberg, who was so **gaunt** with mouse-grey curls. Although I had only seen him twice I would recognize him again anywhere at any time. It was only the colour of his eyes that I was not sure about. We did look into each other's eyes yesterday at the till in the supermarket, but I couldn't say exactly whether Tom had green or blue eyes. Or green-blue perhaps?

Maybe he had the same colour eyes as his mother; he must have inherited something from her, after all. So I did my best to find out the colour of Dr Caberg's eyes behind her **tinted** glasses, but I did not have much success, unfortunately.

"Why are you staring at Caberg like that all the time?" Tanja whispered to me.

I waited for the right moment and whispered back: "Do you think she's got blue eyes?"

Tanja stared at me blankly. "Huh? Bl-bl-**black eye**? Did you say black eye? D'you reckon she got into a fight?" she whispered. Poor Tanja, I thought. She'll probably need a **hearing aid** one of these days. Anyway, our conversation had now finally attracted Caberg's attention.

---

resemblance – Ähnlichkeit; gaunt – hager; tinted – getönt; black eye – blaues Auge, Veilchen; hearing aid – Hörgerät

"Perhaps the ladies sitting in the last row but one would be so good as to follow what I'm saying. If it is within their mental capacity, of course," she said in her high-pitched voice. "If not, they can go and find the kindergarten just two streets away." Of course, there were a couple of **creeps** in the class who **roared** at this lame joke. That seemed to encourage Caberg. With a wave of her hand she summoned me to the blackboard to finish off the calculation.

Easy-peasy, I thought to myself on the way to the front, and was just going to snatch up the piece of chalk and start scribbling away, when I suddenly remembered in time that I'm in desperate need of extra tuition. This was my biggest chance. Caberg could still regard my miserable test as a bit of a **blunder**. But, counting all the homework I had not done, combined with the complete inability that I was about to demonstrate in front of the whole class at the blackboard, it should now become **apparent** to a teacher such as Caberg that things could not go on like this any more.

I stood next to her, wiped the blackboard a bit with the sponge, and was silent.

Caberg was silent, too.

The class became restless in the benches behind me.

---

creep – Schleimer; to roar – grölen; blunder – Ausrutscher; apparent – offensichtlich

Zeynep muttered something, and Dr Caberg looked at her **sternly**. "There'll be no whispering of answers here!"

Zeynep needn't have bothered because she was completely wrong anyway. All the same, it was nice of her to try to help me.

"Well, Henriette?" Dr Caberg's voice had a metallic **ring** to it. She pulled her red notebook out of her well-worn handbag, opened it up and shook her head. "Henriette, I'll give you exactly three minutes to solve the problem!"

I scribbled a series of numbers on the blackboard that didn't make any sense at all. The chalk screeched and several in the class groaned in an undertone. I didn't know whether it was because of the chalk or my calculation.

Satisfied, I took one step back and **scrutinized** my work before I underlined the result with a double line. For a pupil who was actually supposed to be taking part in a nationwide competition for maths in the near future, this was quite a remarkable achievement. Only a candidate for a grade F could possibly make such a **botch-up**.

You could hear Caberg draw in her breath. "Do you really want to leave it like that?" she asked in disbelief.

Of course, I would have preferred to have wiped

---

sternly – streng; ring – Klang; to scrutinize – mustern; botch-up – Pfusch, Murks away all the nonsense that I had written and worked out the correct solution. I would have done it in two minutes, as the problem was not all that difficult, I thought.

"Henriette, do you really want to leave it like that?" repeated Caberg.

I took a deep breath and nodded.

Caberg shook her head in bewilderment and sat down behind the desk. She put the notebook back into her handbag.

"I'll talk to you during the main break. Wait outside the **staff room** for me," she said in a low voice and sent me back to my seat. "Karola, come to the front and show us how to do the calculation properly."

I can't remember what happened for the rest of the lesson. I only know that I kept saying to myself that it was all for the sake of Tom. Once we had become friends I would admit to Caberg that I had only been acting.

Promptly at break time, I was standing in front of the staff room. Caberg came out a few minutes later, carrying a cup of coffee in her hand, and said we should go to the **student council** room where we would be undisturbed.

"Well, Henriette?"

The same question for the second time that day.

---

staff room – Lehrerzimmer; student council – SMV

What was I supposed to reply? I shrugged my shoulders and tried to determine the colour of Caberg's eyes **close-up**. She probably realized that she would not get much information out of me, as she now proceeded to give me a long **lecture**. My poor work over the past few weeks was very clearly the result of adolescent laziness. It was quite normal, of course, for girls of my age to develop new interests – too right, Dr Caberg, I thought to myself. Your son, for example – but it was a crying shame to waste a mathematical talent such as myself. The deterioration would not be all that noticeable in the half-yearly **report** as I still had the grade A's to fall back on from previous tests. But by the summer at the latest, then the former top pupil would have to recognize that she was in danger of not reaching the **required standard**, and all because her head was full of a lot of modern nonsense.

Wait a moment, I wanted to protest. You can't call your son a lot of modern nonsense, but I decided to keep quiet and put on a serious face.

"What shall I do then?" I asked when Dr Caberg was silent for a moment.

She looked at me in amazement and removed her glasses. Now! Now I could see her eyes at last. Unfortunately though, Dr Caberg closed them again immediately. I could see from the vertical **furrow**

---

close-up – aus der Nähe; lecture – Vortrag; report – Zeugnis; required standard – hier: Klassenziel; furrow – Falte

between her eyebrows that she was thinking hard. I didn't dare to say anything else.

After a few seconds she put her glasses back on and said resolutely: "It is simply a question of hard work. Just do some revision and **knuckle down** to work, that's all you need to do, dear Henriette."

She had already turned to the door when I realized that only a frontal attack could help me now. "But that's what I've been doing all the time," I protested. "But there are probably too many gaps now, and nobody can really explain it all to me. Do you think I should take extra tuition?"

There! Now I'd said it, the big word. Caberg had half opened the door, but now closed it again and turned towards me. "Yes, that would be a good idea, certainly. Do it!"

"But my parents are against it!" I said.

Caberg looked at me **aghast**. "But why?" she asked shocked. "There is no real shame in having extra tuition these days. There are some parents who let their children have extra tuition *before* they even start having problems at school. Or is it because of the money?"

I looked uncertain. "I don't know. They don't believe I'm having any real difficulties. And my father says it's hard to find a good teacher, someone who knows exactly what my problems are."

---

to knuckle down – sich dahinter klemmen;
aghast – entgeistert

For the first time that day Caberg smiled at me. "Henriette, we'll **work it out**. I'll call your parents and talk to them. Don't worry, I'll be very careful about it."

I **beamed** a little when I thanked Dr Caberg. "It would be best to ring up this very evening as both my parents are at home," I added, and wrote our telephone number down on a piece of paper.

"I *do* have your number," Caberg said, but I wanted to be on the safe side. My plan was not going to fail simply because Caberg couldn't find our telephone number amongst all her chaos.

Everything was working out **marvellously**. Caberg would ring up to explain to my parents that I was in danger of having to repeat the class.

I hurried into the class room taking large steps. The next lesson had already begun, and everyone was looking at me **in anticipation** when I swung open the door. To get a ticking-off from Caberg was regarded as one of the worst punishments in our school, and our English teacher looked at me rather sympathetically when I explained to him that I'd been kept back. Someone from the class must have told him what had happened.

"Well?" Tanja wanted to know as I sat down.

"Caberg is going to ring up my parents," I mumbled. "But I'll work it out."

---

to work sth out – etwas hinkriegen; to beam – strahlen; marvellously – wunderbar; in anticipation – erwartungsvoll

Should I prepare my parents for the phone call, or not? That was the question that I was thinking about all afternoon. No, it would be better to leave them fully unprepared, I decided **after great length**. It will be much more of a shock that way, and they are then more likely to agree and give their **blessing** to everything. I hadn't felt so good in ages.

The only stupid thing was that Anette was home again. She is twenty-two and works as a laboratory assistant. Actually, she was living together with her boyfriend, but she'd been having quite a lot of trouble with him over the last few days.

"Robert is simply impossible," she complained at supper.

It was the same old story. We always had to hear about Robert's faults, and what demands he made, etc, etc. It was a sickening subject. Mum was the only one who was listening with one ear, Dad was just minding his own business, reading a computer magazine, and I was **dwelling on my thoughts**.

"Robert is totally unable to communicate. You can't have a proper conversation with him," my sister declared, circling her fork over the cheese before she chose the thickest slice of Gouda. "He only ever says yes and no. That's no basis for a relationship. And what's more ..."

I was not to find out what other problems Anette

---

after great length – nach langem Nachdenken;
blessing – Segen; to dwell on one's thoughts – seinen Gedanken nachhängen

had with Robert because the telephone rang. I jumped up. Dr Caberg had kept her word. I had refrained from making my usual phone call to Tanja; I didn't want to block the line under any circumstances. Before I picked up the receiver I looked in the mirror and put on an extremely sad face. That would be **reflected** in my voice, or so I'd read somewhere, and I wanted Caberg to notice how upset I was, and how important it was for me to find someone good for extra tuition.

But I could have saved myself the **bother**. It was the uncommunicative Robert on the phone who asked me yet again whether I'd grown any more lately, and would it be possible to talk to my sister. It wouldn't be a long conversation, I hoped, and thrust the receiver into Anette's hand. If Robert only ever said yes and no, then the phone call would be over in no time at all. But while my sister had been away it seemed that he had recovered from his **disinclination** to talk: the pair of them were talking to each other for a whole hour.

Finally, even Dad noticed how nervous I was. "What's up with our little one?" he asked my mother.

"No problems please," said Mum. "We've got enough on our plate with Anette. I wanted to turn her bedroom into a study because I thought she and

---

to reflect – sich widerspiegeln; bother – Mühe; disinclination – Unlust

Robert were a **fixed item**. Do you think it will turn out alright again?"

"Well, they are talking to each other again," said Dad happily. "I bet they'll still be on the phone at one o'clock this morning'.

I could feel how I turned quite **pale**. Anette and her stupid Robert were **jeopardizing** my love life, because I very much doubted whether Caberg would want to listen to the **engaged tone** all evening again tomorrow.

"Hey, Dad," I shouted, "someone rang up about the monitor."

That was my last hope. Two weeks ago Dad had put in an advertisement for an old computer monitor which nobody had taken any interest in as yet, apart from a **retired** railway official who wanted to know whether he would be able to read timetables in small print on it. But the man had rung a week ago, and I had just forgotten to tell Dad about it.

"When did somebody ring up?" he wanted to know right away.

I had to tell a **white lie**. About midday, I claimed, and he would now be trying to get through this very moment, but of course the line was engaged through Anette's call, and …

That had the desired effect. Dad stood up and marched into Anette's room. He didn't have to say

---

fixed item – etwas Festes; pale – blass;
to jeopardize – gefährden; engaged tone – Besetztzeichen;
retired – im Ruhestand; white lie – Notlüge

much, she willingly ended the conversation. After all, it's not easy talking to your sweetheart when one of your parents is sitting in the background listening.

"Well?" asked Mum expectantly when Anette sat back down to supper. "Everything OK?"

Anette **scoffed**. "You've got to be joking. You just can't talk to Robert."

Well, at least it took her a whole hour and thirteen minutes to find that out.

"I think I'll come back home. **For the time being**, at least, until I can find my own flat. And I can take care of Henriette a bit, and help out in the household every now and again."

Help out in the household every now and again. What a laugh! In the past, Anette's help in the household was usually **confined to** giving out orders for the servant, the servant being me, of course.

Dad was about to say something, but the phone rang and he answered immediately. I could tell who he was talking to by the worried look on his face. I think he'd had quite enough of his daughters' problems that evening. But at least my problems could be **remedied** simply with extra tuition, whereas Anette could not be helped quite as easily.

"I'll talk to my wife about it and let you know," he said finally and grimaced in pain. When he had

---

to scoff – spöttisch lachen; for the time being – erst mal, vorübergehend; to be confined to – sich beschränken auf; to remedy – behandeln

put the phone down he rubbed his left ear. "Does your maths teacher always shout like that during lessons? It sounded like she was trying to silence a **hoard** of noisy juniors by screaming at them," he sighed.

"Dr Caberg?" inquired my mother. She seemed to be rather worried now. "At this time? What did she want then?"

Dad looked at me with concern. He then sighed. "She says that things are not looking too good for Henriette in maths at the moment. Well, that's a bit of an **understatement**. Our daughter's performance in class is quite catastrophic. Caberg says we shouldn't worry too much about the reasons. In her opinion, the only solution would be extra tuition straight away so that the gaps don't get even wider, and Henri can return to her old form."

"Extra tuition. Well then!" My mother looked rather tired as she said that. "If it's possible to get rid of the problem as simply as that, then, alright, I don't mind. And *who* is supposed to give her tuition?"

"What about Babette?" asked my sister. "It's about time she took care of her youngest sister, too. Babette's got the best life out of all of us. I'd like to study, too."

If you'd paid more attention in English, then you would have got your Abitur, too, I felt like saying, but

---

hoard – Horde; understatement – Untertreibung

I stopped myself. I didn't want Anette to become my enemy.

"But Babette only comes home at the weekend, and I don't think that's enough, is it?" I said, and Dad **backed me up**. "Caberg suggests twice a week at least, otherwise it would be useless. By the way, she praised the fact that you're interested in having extra tuition yourself. In her opinion, that is the precondition for improving your performance."

"And who is now going to give Henri extra tuition?" my mother wanted to know.

"Dr Caberg," I said quickly before Anette thought of offering to help me. "After all, she knows best what I've got to learn!"

Dad laughed. "Yes, and then she'll give you **hints** for the next test." He shook his head. "No, no, she said straight away on the phone that she can't give you tuition herself, even if she wanted to. But she will look for a good teacher for you."

I think I had a pretty stupid look on my face at that moment. Blast! I hadn't expected something like this. Perhaps I would soon be sitting opposite a retired senior teacher, listening to him **reminiscing** about school as it used to be. Twice a week. Blast, blast, and triple blast! I had to ring up Tanja and tell her all about it. Perhaps she knew of some way out of this ridiculous situation.

---

to back sb up – jmd. unterstützen; hint – Tipp, Hinweis;
to reminisce – in Erinnerungen schwelgen

"Don't be too long on the phone, Robert might ring up again," Anette begged me as I was about to disappear into my room with the phone in my hand.

"And the man who's interested in the monitor will also probably want to **get in touch**," yelled Dad, but I was already closing the door. I had enough problems of my own, let everyone else see to themselves.

Tanja didn't sound **particularly** pleased when I rang. The television was on loud in the background. "I'm just watching a brilliant film," she told me. "The leading actor is called Stewart Mellary, and he lives in Los Angeles. I've found out that much so far. The film is about the secret of a …"

"I've also got a secret to tell you," I said in my darkest voice. You had to **resort** to such methods with Tanja sometimes. She promptly **turned** the television **down**, and said: "OK. But only ten minutes. I'll have to switch over then. I don't want to miss the interview with Stewart, under any circumstances." I couldn't expect any real help from Tanja, but all the same it did me good to tell her everything.

"I thought as much," she said **after great length**. "It was all a bit strange. I mean, me being better than you at maths, all of a sudden. But I'd never have thought you were **capable** of that. It's really romantic. Like in a film!"

---

to get in touch – Kontakt aufnehmen; particularly – besonders; to resort – Zuflucht nehmen; to turn down – leiser stellen; after great length – nach längerem Nachdenken; capable – fähig

"But it's not all that romantic at the moment, sadly. I'm faced with the prospect of extra tuition, either with a retired old teacher, or my sister, and that will be dreadful," I said. "I've got to find another way of getting to know Tom Caberg. Any ideas?"

For the next hour we discussed all the possibilities. Tanja was so enthusiastic about the whole thing that she didn't even think about her new favourite actor or his interview any more. Unfortunately, though, we didn't come up with one single useful idea.

"I can look up your horoscope," my friend said finally. "You're **Libra**, aren't you?"

Tanja **rummaged through** a pile of glossy magazines, muttering from time to time, "Damn, where is it now", and at last found what she was looking for. **Spellbound** she studied the magazine "Stargazer."

"Well?" I asked. Actually, I didn't believe in horoscopes, but for a moment I was unsure. Perhaps …

"Nothing important," reckoned Tanja, "I mean, nothing that would get us any further."

"Go on, read it out," I asked her.

"Alright then. As you wish," said Tanja, and then read out the most awful horoscope ever: 'Venus is not at her best at present. It is a bad time for matters of the heart.' Do you want to hear any more?"

I swallowed. "Yeah. I don't believe in it, anyway."

Libra – Waage; to rummage through – durchstöbern; spellbound – gebannt

"Then why am I reading all this out to you in the first place," Tanja complained. "But alright, if that's what you want. 'Expect a number of surprises very soon that will **require** great understanding on your part. Stay optimistic! It's all in your own hands.'"

"And what does that mean exactly?" I inquired. "Does it mean that Caberg will be giving me extra tuition after all?"

Tanja mumbled disapprovingly. She explained that you mustn't take horoscopes **literally**, but you could be one hundred percent sure that there was always some truth in them. Take her horoscope, for example, she should be making plans **on a greater scale**, it said, and that's why she was convinced that Stewart Mellary was the right one for her.

I interrupted her hastily. "But that doesn't get me anywhere now. What would you do in my place?"

"Just ring him up, and tell him that you think he's nice," Tanja suggested after thinking for a long while.

I swallowed. "Would you do something like that?"

She thought about it for a short moment. "If I find out the address of Stewart, and his phone number, then I'll ring him up. That'll be difficult, of course, because he only understands English. So *you* can ring up *Tom*, with no problem!"

I hesitated. "But what if he laughs, or something?

---

to require – erfordern; literally – wörtlich;
on a greater scale – in größeren Dimensionen

And what's my reason for ringing him up in the first place? I can't just say I think you're really nice. Anyway, he doesn't even know me."

We were both silent. Tanja turned up the television again. "Maybe I'll think of something better," she said finally. "Let's talk about it in school tomorrow."

When I returned the phone to the hallway, someone was ringing the doorbell **incessantly**. Robert was standing there with a bright red face, looking pretty **shattered**. "Damn, Henri, who's been on the phone all the time?" he inquired. "I've been trying to get in touch with Anette for nearly two hours, but all I ever hear is beep – beep – beep." He twisted his mouth. "Where on earth is your sister? I've got a lot to say to her."

For someone who is supposed to be totally uncommunicative, Robert was talking quite a lot, I thought. I gestured towards the living room where I **suspected** my sister to be, and grinned. Have fun with your problems, I thought as I went to bed.

"I hope you are aware, Henriette, that **proper** extra tuition is an expensive business," my mother greeted me at breakfast the next morning.

I nodded. That had to come. Three daughters, one studying, one earning, although needing twice

---

incessantly – unaufhörlich; shattered – am Boden zerstört; to suspect – vermuten; proper – gut, richtig, anständig

as much, and another one still at school. And these young ladies were very demanding: always wanting new clothes, trainers, etc, etc. It was the same old story.

But mum did not get very far with her complaint, because Dad noted that Anette had gone back to Robert. "The pair of them were talking half the night, and I could hardly get to sleep," he complained. "Oh well, at least they seem to be **getting on** with each other again."

Until the next time, I would have liked to have foretold, until my sister discovers once again that her Robert is not able to communicate. My temper that morning had dropped to well below **freezing point**, because I had come to realize that there would be no more little extras, like an **allowance** for a special pair of trainers for example, because of the expense of extra tuition.

On the way into the classroom I ran straight into Caberg. "How fortunate that I see you," she said. "I have found somebody for you."

I nodded **humbly**. I had to go through with it now, I only had myself to blame.

"I tried to ring your father up at least three times last night, but your telephone was always engaged. Or you hadn't replaced the receiver properly."

I nodded again.

---

to get on – sich verstehen; freezing point – Gefrierpunkt; allowance – Zuschuss; humbly – ergeben

"You know, of course, that I am not allowed to give you extra tuition, unfortunately. But I have found someone who is really talented and who is also good at teaching. Please don't go **shouting it all about**! My son is already giving lessons to one pupil, and two is the absolute limit. He won't have enough time for himself, otherwise."

"Your son?" I desperately needed somewhere to sit down. "Your son is going to give me extra tuition?"

Caberg looked at me somewhat worried. "Yes. Isn't that alright with you? He's two classes above you, and is very talented. If there are ever any problems, I'm always nearby, and he can then discuss them with me."

"Oh, no, that's OK," I exclaimed. "I just didn't understand you. I mean, I didn't **catch** what you said. I think I'll have to go and see an ear specialist." I laughed stupidly.

I was unable to think clearly for the moment. Tom Caberg would be giving me extra tuition. It was like scoring a **brilliant goal**! All my trouble had been worth it. I nearly flung my arms around Caberg, but I then realized it may raise some suspicions if I were to be too enthusiastic about the prospect of extra tuition.

I smiled **amiably** when Caberg gave me a note with her address on it, and gave me my first appointment:

---

to shout sth all about – etwas überall herumerzählen;
to catch – hier: verstehen; brilliant goal – Volltreffer;
amiably – freundlich

"Thursday at half-past two. Please be punctual, and don't forget!"

Don't forget! I couldn't think about anything other than Thursday at half-past two. It meant that I wouldn't be able to go to football training, but one does have to make small sacrifices.

In my best mood ever, I walked into the classroom ten minutes after the lesson had begun. "Dr Caberg had to talk to me about something," I apologized to the English teacher.

I was met with sympathetic looks from my fellow pupils. Poor Henri! Caberg *does* really seem **to have it in for** her, some of them probably thought.

Tanja nodded to me. "I've thought something out. A plan. You know," she whispered.

"Everything's OK," I muttered. "I'm having extra tuition with Tom Caberg!"

---

to have it in for sb – jmd. auf dem Kieker haben

I was floating

on clouds. Life was wonderful, and from tomorrow onwards it would be even more wonderful. Thursday, half-past two, Luisenstr. 16, please be punctual. I could have kissed Caberg's note. But Tanja brought me back to earth with a **bump**.

"What are you going to wear?" she inquired on the way home.

I looked at her in amazement.

"Well, I mean, you do want to catch Tom, don't you?" When she looked at my **blank** face, she laughed. "I'll come over to your place this afternoon and bring a few magazines with me. We can think of something then. Remember, the **competition** is tough."

The competition is tough. I couldn't get that silly sentence out of my head. I hadn't thought about it from *that* **angle**. I had naturally assumed that I would

---

bump – Plumps; blank – verständnislos;
competition – Konkurrenz; angle – Blickwinkel

only have to sit opposite Tom, and he'd fall in love with me **straight away**. Maybe Tanja knows a bit more about these things. She's seen loads of films, knows all the magazines, and she wears make-up, too.

On the way home I could only see really attractive girls and young women, all of a sudden. They were all fantastically dressed, had make-up on, and had their hair **dyed**. I hardly dared think what I looked like.

Of course, the first thing I saw when I got home was the large mirror in the hallway. I just had to examine myself closer. I smiled at myself, grinned, pulled faces, but I was still the same old Henriette: light brown hair, blue eyes, thirteen freckles, a nose that was a little bit too small, and a teeny-weeny little gap between the teeth. Well, if I didn't open my mouth too much, you couldn't see it at all. And what about the rest of me? I hastily pulled off my jeans and sweatshirt, and turned myself in front of the mirror. Not much of a **bust** yet, but that would develop at some time or other, no doubt. The **calves of my legs**, well, they were what you would call real footballer's legs. It wasn't for nothing that I'd scored the most goals in the last half year. Actually, I was not altogether dissatisfied. I smiled at my reflection, blew some kisses and did a little dance. Just at that moment, the front door opened and my mother was

---

straight away – auf der Stelle, sofort; to dye – färben;
bust – Busen; calves of the legs – Waden

standing there in the hallway, loaded down with bags and packages.

She stared at me **in bewilderment**. "Henriette, what are you doing? Why have you taken your clothes off? Are you ill?"

I grabbed my clothes, pulled the **jumper** over my head and tried to think of a good reason why I was dancing around the flat half naked at two o'clock in the afternoon. "My arms and legs were itching so much," I said finally while Mum was still looking at me with concern. "Well, I thought I might have the **measles** or something."

"And? Do you?

I shook my head. "No, don't worry. Everything is OK."

"How did maths go today? Any better?"

I shook my head and pulled on my jeans. "No, but Caberg has found a teacher for me, and besides, I'm just going to say I can't go to the next football training session."

My mother looked pleased. "I'm glad that you're beginning **to see sense**, Henriette," she said. "All this football playing wasn't right for you. When your maths marks have improved again you can start taking riding lessons. That's a great thing for girls, isn't it?

I nodded. Riding lessons! You've got to be kid-

---

in bewilderment – fassungslos; jumper – Pulli;
measles – Masern; to see sense – zur Vernunft kommen

ding. I was afraid of horses; but who'd ever heard of a football that **thrashes about**. But that was not interesting for the moment. Much more important was the fact that I was having extra tuition with Tom Caberg.

"And who has the good Dr Caberg found for you?" inquired Mum.

When she heard that Caberg's son would be giving me tuition, she looked doubtful. "I don't know," she said after a while, "will it be really worthwhile? I mean, if he's only two years older than you and …"

"Oh Mum, it's just as if Caberg would be giving me tuition herself," I interrupted her. Besides, it would look rather silly if I cancelled it now. It would be as if we didn't think her son was qualified."

Mum **admitted defeat**. "Well, if that's what you think," she said half convinced. "I'll have a talk to Dr Caberg later, to discuss the money as well."

"I'll put something towards it," I offered. The plan shouldn't fail just because of money.

Mum smiled. "It's alright. I'll take you up on your offer if necessary."

Tanja turned up in the afternoon, carrying at least five magazines in her school bag.

"Oh, are you going to do some work?" asked Mum pleased. "Just say if you need any help."

---

to thrash about – um sich treten;
to admit defeat – sich geschlagen geben

By the time we'd **flicked through** the third magazine, Tanja had also come to realize that we were not going to be able to transform me into one of these girlies overnight.

"If you could at least dye your hair red? Or how about a little diamond in your nose?" my friend finally suggested. "I mean, that doesn't really take a lot of **effort**."

Dyeing my hair, diamond in my nose! "And how am I going to explain that to my parents? D'you think they'll allow something like that?"

Tanja laughed. "Well, my mother asked me if I'd like a diamond for my nose. Guess what, she might even get herself pierced!"

I **shuddered** at the very idea of having a hole pierced in my lip or eyebrow, but I didn't tell Tanja that. I don't think I could have anything like that done, not even for the love of Tom.

Besides, there is one small but **crucial** difference between Tanja's mother and my parents: Dad usually goes around in a suit and tie, and Mum wears a suit, in the office at least. In comparison, Tanja's mother goes around in silver-coloured leggings and platform shoes. It was my hard luck if Tom was into rings in noses and all that stuff. I tried to think whether he had been wearing an earring, but I couldn't remember. I could also hardly imagine Caberg allowing her

---

to flick through – durchblättern; effort – Aufwand;
to shudder – erschaudern; crucial – entscheidend

son to wear one. But then again, he might find girls with nose rings particularly interesting for that very reason. I sighed, and Tanja punched me in the side to cheer me up. Feeling frustrated I flicked through the next glossy magazine until at last I found the article that helped me.

"Hey, Tanja, look. It says here in a survey that boys **attach importance** to inner values such as loyalty, reliability, honesty ..."

Oh dear, I'd been fibbing quite a lot lately, but loyal, yes, I could be that, and reliable too.

Tanja laughed unpleasantly. "Huh, inner values. That's what my mother believed until my father came along with his girlfriend. What a lot of good inner values were for my mother. But there you are. If that's what you **reckon**. I was only trying to help." Tanja gathered the magazines together **in** rather **a huff**.

"By the way, I heard something about Stewart on the radio yesterday," I lied.

That was stupid, I'd fibbed again! But I couldn't afford to have any trouble with Tanja. If we really had a serious **argument**, and she told everyone in the class all about it all, what would happen then? I could feel myself going red. Everyone would laugh at me. Henriette has fallen in love with Caberg's son, and is putting on a big show. No, I couldn't have any

---

to attach importance – Wert legen auf; to reckon – meinen, einschätzen; in a huff – eingeschnappt; argument – Streit

arguments with Tanja. Starting tomorrow, I would be completely honest again, I decided.

Unfortunately, Tanja was only moderately interested in Stewart. "He lives in Los Angeles, and I won't be going there in the near future," she explained to me. "Anyway, for the last six days there's been a series on the television in the early evening with Ronald Reiman, and he looks a bit like Stewart. Ronald lives in Berlin, and it won't be all that difficult to find out his address."

I promised my friend to try and find out Ronald Reimann's address, to watch the seventh episode of "Heidhoferstraße, 4th floor", and to ring up Tanja straight away to let her know what I thought of Ronald.

"Perhaps I'll think of something for tomorrow," she said half-**reconciled** when she went home shortly afterwards. "And don't forget: half-past six, channel 1."

Reliability. One of those inner values again! I was determined to watch the "Heidhoferstraße" at half-past six and ring up Tanja afterwards. How could I have known that Anette would turn up just in time for supper, blocking the living room for a whole hour?

She needed to have a chat with Mum about Robert, who had behaved **abominably** and proved to be completely unable to communicate, yet again.

---

reconciled – versöhnt; abominably – abscheulich

When I carefully **poked** my head into the room just after half-past six, and asked whether I could watch something on television, she snapped at me, as if I'd been Robert. I shouldn't watch too much television and I would do better to learn maths, and anyway, it was her future **at stake** here, etc., etc. My mother gave me a sign, indicating that it was much more serious than the last time, so I closed the door and had to miss Ronald Reimann.

"Well, weren't you going to ring me up?" Tanja said nastily as I walked into the classroom.

I had especially taken a later tram so as not to meet her on the way to school.

"Did you watch 'Heidhoferstraße' or not?"

I wanted to be honest, starting from today. Besides, it would have been extremely difficult to lie in this particular case because I hadn't ever heard or seen anything about this series before.

"My sister is having trouble with her Robert again. She blocked the living room the whole evening," I said truthfully, but Tanja just **scoffed**.

"Huh, and I'm supposed to believe that?"

I was silent.

"You're just not interested in the really important things in life," she went on. "But just to show you that I am a true friend, I've brought you something. It's

---

to poke – hier: stecken, strecken; to be at stake – auf dem Spiel stehen; to scoff – spöttisch lachen

my mother's." With a mysterious look, she handed me a spray. "**Copper** red. Looks really cool. You've just got to spray it on your hair. You can wash it out again in the evening."

I thanked her enthusiastically, and hoped that my voice sounded fairly **genuine**. I would definitely watch "Heidhoferstraße" that evening, and I was determined to find the series fantastic, especially Ronald Reimann.

I was supposed to be in Luisenstraße at half-past two **on the dot**. A ten minutes' walk and a quarter of an hour on the tram. I had to leave home by two at the latest. Time would be a bit short because I wanted to change the way I looked just a bit. With all her talk of tough competition, Tanja had put a stupid idea in my head. I'd been having a close look at the girls from my class all morning. I'd never noticed before how many of them were dressed in the latest fashion. But there were also a few who were just wearing jeans and a jumper or blouse, like me. And which type did the boys of our class go for? The trendy ones, of course. Mind you, the boys in our class were anything but attractive: most of them had **pimples** and greasy hair. It was hardly any wonder that Tanja fell for actors instead, and I for Tom.

When I got home, I washed my hair and **smoth-**

---

copper – Kupfer; genuine – echt; on the dot – Punkt (14.30 Uhr); pimple – Pickel; to smother – schmieren

ered some of Mum's day cream on my face. "With lifting effect" it said. I certainly didn't have any wrinkles, but I couldn't find any other decent cream in the bathroom, and I definitely didn't want to use the hand cream that reeked of camomile.

What should I wear? Three pairs of jeans, a **checked pleated skirt** that I last wore to my grandparents' golden wedding anniversary, seven sweatshirts (four second-hand, and three new ones) and three pullovers – that was the total sum of my belongings in the wardrobe. Then there was a football kit and two **track-suits**. Jeans, well, they were OK, but all of a sudden I didn't like my sweatshirts any more. I thought they made me look like a **gangling** twelve-year old. And I was almost fourteen. Looking younger is a family trait; even my sisters look younger than they actually are. Looking from behind, you could easily mistake Anette for me, and she's eight years older than me, after all. Precisely! Why hadn't I thought of it straight away? Mum had bought a terrific dark blue mohair jumper for her daughter Anette who was causing her a bit of worry. It was supposed to be as a **small consolation** because of Robert, because the pair of them were serious about splitting up in the meantime. That jumper would suit me really well. Anyway, I'd deserved a consolation, too.

---

checked pleated skirt – karierter Faltenrock;
track-suit – Trainingsanzug; gangling – schlaksig;
small consolation – Trostpflaster

Feeling only slightly guilty, I sneaked into my sister's room, took the new jumper out of the cupboard and tried it on. Just as I thought – it fitted me perfectly and looked really fantastic. I now just had to be careful not to let Mum catch me.

I **crept** back into the hallway **on tip-toe** and put my anorak on over the top. Today's post was lying on the hall stand: on the top there was a flyer. "Give pleasure this Christmas," was written on it, and underneath: "A new fragrance is always a welcome gift."

Of course! Why hadn't I thought of it straight away? When the perfumery in Tanja's road had a **clearance sale**, I had stocked up with Christmas presents: half-price perfumes. I had hidden Mum's in my desk. After searching for a long time I had the bottle in my hand. Should I, or shouldn't I? I looked at myself critically in a pocket mirror. Yeah, something was missing. If I didn't have a ring in my nose, or red-dyed hair, then perfume was the very least I should have. Making a quick decision, I opened the bottle and **dabbed** some of it behind my ears, just like Mum and Anette. I felt that I reeked of perfume at first, but the fragrance faded quickly. To be on the safe side, I splashed some more on my hair. And maybe I should spray a red strand in my hair, after all? I'd seen one of the other pupils doing it in the

---

to creep on tip-toe – auf Zehenspitzen schleichen; clearance sale – Räumungsverkauf; to dab – tupfen

school yard, and thought it looked like a bit of fun. And it would definitely please Tanja, anyway. With the spray in my hand, I closed my eyes and sprayed it around my head a bit. Well, you couldn't see much, but that was **just as well**. Besides, there wasn't much I could do about it, anyway, as it was just before two and I had to leave.

On the way to Luisenstraße I felt like a different person. In appearance, anyway. My hair had a few red tints, and I was wearing a new mohair jumper underneath my anorak. And what's more, I was stinking of perfume. But I felt different on the inside, too: more **mature**, more grown-up. A few girls in my class already had a boyfriend. Evelyn for example. She bragged about it an awful lot. Every other sentence started with: "My Matthias says ..." He was supposedly going to give her an **engagement** ring for Christmas. That was absolutely ridiculous, according to Tanja. Last weekend Matthias had been ice-skating with Christiane, and that looked more like an engagement. There was probably no-one in my class who thought I was capable of a steady boyfriend. Firstly because I was the youngest, and secondly because I was only interested in football, anyway.

I planned not to be seen with Tom until we'd known each other for a few weeks. Perhaps he would

---

just as well – ganz gut so; mature – reif;
engagement – Verlobung

pick me up from school. Too bad that I hadn't asked Caberg which school her son went to. Perhaps he finished earlier than me and could then wait for me at the school gate. Wouldn't I like to see Saskia's face then. Two months ago we had been doing love poems in German, and when I put my hand up in class, the silly cow had laughed and said I wouldn't know anything about that. I was looking forward to seeing their faces when they saw me together with Tom. Especially when they see that we are going together.

If I hurry I can still **knit** a scarf for Tom for Christmas, I thought to myself, with our initials on it. That's nearly as good as an engagement ring, at least for the beginning. It was a pity that I hated knitting. But I could ask my Grandma to knit me a scarf. I would then **iron** on the initials, just like patches on jeans. Better still, I could ask for two identical scarves from Grandma, to make it even more obvious that Tom and I belong together. I decided to write to my Grandma straight away.

And how will my parents react? Tom looks pretty normal, in fact. No hair dyed yellow, and no safety-pin through his cheek or anything like that. That's what Anette's second boyfriend looked like, you see, the one before Robert. And the first one had been a complete disaster: twenty years older than Anette, newly divorced and a **sparse** amount of hair on the

---

to knit – stricken; to iron – bügeln; sparse – spärlich

back of his head. I smiled: my parents could be satisfied with my choice.

Three minutes before half-past two I was standing in front of the entrance to Luisenstraße number 16. I scrutinized the old grey four-storey building. I suddenly did not feel all that well, in fact I was feeling pretty sick. At the last second I had thought of a few subjects to talk about apart from maths. I hope he's a bit interested in football, I thought; at least I wouldn't start **stammering** stupidly on that subject.

There's **no chickening out** now, Henriette, I said to myself as I studied the nameplates. Jennifer Tschabulli, I read, Charlotte Wolter, then a bell without a name, and right at the top in Caberg's typical **scribble**: Renate Caberg, Dietmar Caberg. Look, so there was a Mr Caberg after all. Who had actually **spread the rumour** that Caberg was divorced? At half-past two on the dot I rang the bell.

The Cabergs lived on the fourth floor. Thank heavens that my sport kept me in top form. Tanja would certainly have been completely out of breath by the time she reached the top floor.

My maths teacher opened the door. "Punctual, very punctual," she noted **appreciatively**. "Come along here to the **study**. My son will be there in a minute. Have you brought the money with you?" She

---

to stammer – stottern; no chickening out – Kneifen gilt nicht; scribble – Gekritzel; to spread a rumour – ein Gerücht verbreiten; appreciatively – anerkennend; study – Arbeitszimmer

counted the money that I'd taken out of an envelope, smiled encouragingly and left the room.

I looked around curiously. Firstly because it's always funny to see how teachers live, and secondly because I was particularly interested because of Tom. The study did not make a very **cosy** impression: it was long and narrow like a tube, and was crammed full with old cupboards. There was a wide table in front of the window with a pale yellow tablecloth. A desk lamp only gave out little light. I sat down on an orange-coloured plastic chair and **dug** out my papers from the rucksack. Well, to be honest, this study was not meant to make you feel comfortable. I rather felt as though I was in the **junk room**. But what the heck, I thought, I'm not here for the atmosphere, but because I want to get to know Tom at last.

On that particular day Caberg had given us piles of homework to do. On the way to Luisenstraße I had done a few sums and solved the first three problems in ten minutes. To be on the safe side, I had carefully torn up the note with the answers on it and had thrown it into the waste paper bin at the tram stop. I would ask Tom a few intelligent **questions at intervals**, it would take us about twenty minutes to finish the homework, and then we'd still have another twenty minutes to talk to each other.

---

cosy – gemütlich; to dig – hier: kramen; junk room – Rumpelkammer; questions at intervals – Zwischenfragen

I stood up and glanced out of the high, narrow window: it had started to snow outside, and it wasn't much warmer on the inside. I felt the radiator below the window. Luke-warm. I tried to turn it up, but with little success. **It was a good job** that I had my sister's warm mohair jumper on. I would certainly have frozen to death in this icy cold if I had been wearing a sweatshirt.

I heard the door opening behind my back. Now! I turned around, beaming all over my face. I had practiced this smile in bed last night for at least half an hour. I'd got it just right. "A knock-out," Tanja would say when talking about her actor.

But I had done all that beaming for nothing. The boy who walked into the room, armed with a maths book, **folder** and **calculator** was a stranger. He said: "Hallo!"

I stared at him. I was supposed to be having individual tuition, wasn't I? Caberg hadn't mentioned that there would be anyone else here. Under no circumstances was I going to share my Tom with this boring-looking **swot**. His thin, fair-haired curls had been combed with a parting on the right side. Ridiculous!

The **twerp** sat down on the other orange-coloured plastic chair opposite me, smoothed the tablecloth and looked at me impatiently with pale blue eyes. I

---

it's a good job – wie gut, dass ...; folder – Schnellhefter; calculator – Taschenrechner; swot – Streber; twerp – Blödmann

put on an arrogant face and ignored him. If only Tom would come at last!

"Right then, let's get on with it at last," said the person opposite me finally and opened the maths book.

I still didn't say anything, but somehow I had the most awful feeling that something was not quite working out as I'd planned.

"Where should we begin? What have you got for homework?" he repeated.

He sounded even more impatient. It was beginning **to dawn** on me. "Are you giving the lessons?" I asked in disbelief.

He looked at me surprised. "Yes, of course."

"But your brother ...," I started.

He **frowned**. "I haven't got a brother. Maybe I ought to make a formal introduction. I'm Dietmar Caberg. Do you want to see my birth certificate? What are all these questions, anyway?"

It was Dr Caberg's son, of course. You could not overlook the similarity, the same hair and the same face structure. Caberg probably had pale blue eyes, too. I shook my head, **appalled**. How could I have ever thought that Caberg might have a nice son – someone like Tom. It's a well-known fact that the apple doesn't fall far from the tree.

"Right then, can we start now?" Dietmar asked

---

to dawn – dämmern; to frown – die Stirn runzeln;
appalled – entsetzt

once again. “It is your money, after all, and ten minutes have gone already.”

I nodded, pushed my maths exercise book towards him, and wished I was quite far away.

I’d taken all that trouble just for this. My maths marks had **plummeted** dramatically, and I had plenty of problems both at home and in school. My Mum’s Christmas present had been wasted for nothing, and my sister would of course notice that someone had worn her jumper before her. But the worst thing of all was that I had to spend three quarters of an hour with Dietmar Caberg in this unheated junk room which in the meantime reeked horribly of perfume.

I slumped in my chair and listened apathetically while he showed me how to work out one problem after the other. Towards the end of the lesson his mother popped her head around the door, asked whether I had understood everything, and requested her son to open the window pretty quickly. She thought there was an awful smell in the room; hadn’t we noticed the strange smell. She then went on to tell us about the dead mouse that had been lying under the piano in the living room for weeks, and how they’d only found the **carcass** by chance. Dietmar had probably heard this story before because he just went on with his calculations indifferently while I was already starting to feel ill.

---

to plummet – absacken; carcass – Kadaver

"Do you think there might be another dead animal in here, too?" asked Caberg. "Can't you really smell anything?"

Neither Dietmar or I answered. I was to come again next Tuesday, at the same time, and just as punctual, please.

I rushed out of the house. I would have best liked to go straight to Tanja's to **give** her **a piece of my mind**. She had got me into this fine mess. Tom, really. Curly Dietmar was Caberg's son. I should force her to sit through the nine remaining lessons. You see, Caberg had agreed on a "package" of ten lessons with my mother. That was the very least, otherwise it wouldn't be worth all the trouble and effort; after all, her son had to prepare the material and everything. Tanja was now probably sitting in front of the television, **nibbling** peanuts, gazing at good-looking young men and working out the best way of getting to know them.

But instead of going to Tanja's I went straight home. I needed somewhere to cry my eyes out undisturbed. I would tell Tanja about it all afterwards, and finish our friendship unless she had a very good excuse indeed. I arrived home, totally **dejected**.

Dad opened the door for me. "Well, was the first lesson any good?," he greeted me. "You know that you've got **to knuckle down** now, don't you? You'll

---

to give sb a piece of one's mind – jmd. die Meinung sagen; nibbling – knabbern; dejected – geknickt, niedergeschlagen; to knuckle down – sich dahinter klemmen

have to revise everything that young Caberg explained to you. You know, it's only by learning on your own that you can ..."

I sobbed out loud.

Dad looked at me alarmed. "Henri, come on, it's not all that bad. It'll turn out alright in the end. You've got maths in your blood, believe me. This is only **temporary**." I had no idea why I was sobbing my heart out, but it was nice being comforted. I sobbed even louder. Dad swallowed. "Alright, you know what I said about your Christmas present, about it being a bit smaller this year because of the extra tuition ... well, forget it. Don't you worry about it."

When I had cried three paper handkerchiefs full, and Dad really didn't know how to comfort me any more, the telephone rang. Tanja! I gave a big sniff and took the telephone into my room. I could **do without** any witnesses to the following conversation.

"I thought I'd ring you up to hear how it went," said Tanja. It was important to her, evidently, because there wasn't the usual noise of the television in the background.

Actually, I wanted **to wipe the floor with** Tanja, but I changed my mind all of a sudden.

"Oh Tanja," I said, wiping the tears from my face. "Tom is really as nice as I'd imagined."

"Oh yes," she said. "And what does he think of you? Have you got red hair now, by the way?"

---

temporary – vorübergehend; to do without – verzichten;
to wipe the floor with sb – jmd. fertig machen

"He thinks I'm great too, I think. Maybe because of my red hair. But the colour has disappeared now, more or less. You probably won't notice anything in school tomorrow."

Tanja swallowed audibly. "Well, now that you're friends with Tom, you won't have time for me anymore. I've got to go now because Ronald Reimann is coming."

"To your place?" I asked in amazement.

She sniffed briefly. "Yeah, to my place. On the first channel!"

For a moment I had the impression that Tanja was crying, too.

I put the receiver down, carefully took off the mohair jumper that was reeking of perfume, returned it to her room, and sat down in front of the television in the living room. The tears were streaming down my face, and I could only see through a **veil** how Ronald Reimann, as a student in "Heidhoferstraße, 4th floor", was solving all the problems.

"Henri's watching a **soap** and is crying her eyes out," I heard Anette say suddenly. Mum and Dad were standing at the door, with a blank look on their faces.

"No more problems, please," begged my mother and switched the television off. "Henriette, it's only a film. The director tells the actors what to do and … Anyway, you're old enough." She looked around helplessly.

---

veil – Schleier; soap – hier: Serie

Dad shook his head. "I don't think she's crying about the film. It's more about the maths extra tuition. I suspect she's worried that she still won't manage the school year."

My mother sat down on the coffee table. Sighing quietly she took off her shoes. She then smiled and said: "Henriette, everything is OK. You're having extra tuition, and we're certainly the last to criticise if the next test still doesn't turn out all that well. So please, Henriette, be a bit more **sensible**."

That made me cry even more, unfortunately. I don't know where the tears came from, I just couldn't stop.

"That must be puberty," said my sister, "that's when you start going crazy. I can remember when I was the same age as Henri. Isn't that when I'd just fallen in love with Norbert or whatever his name was? My God, was I unhappy when he **finished with** me after just two days. He was fourteen then, and I was thirteen." Anette laughed. "That was my first unhappy love, and I thought I'd never fancy anyone again."

I had to sob again. Unfortunately, I'd got a severe attack of the **hiccups** at the same time. Dad brought me a glass of water. "Is that what it is? Are you unhappily in love?"

I shook my head. No-one was going to find out anything about Tom and me.

---

sensible – vernünftig; to finish with sb – mit jmd. Schluss machen; hiccups – Schluckauf

“Look,” said Dad, “Anette survived her unhappy love. You’ll be laughing about it in two weeks.”

That’s typical of so-called grown-ups. Everything is sorted out the next moment. But I’ll never be able to laugh again, I thought, as I threw myself onto the bed in my room. Anette was quick to get over her **lovesickness**, naturally. Well, she does everything else sensibly, too. Anette will never be truly unhappy, and neither will Babette. When life gets tough, she turns to mathematic formulae for comfort. I am the only one in this family who is capable of having any feelings at all, I thought just before I fell asleep.

“We told you that you’d soon get over your lovesickness, didn’t we?” Mum said when I came into the kitchen the next morning, making a relatively normal impression.

I smiled **flatly**, refused any breakfast and ran off to the tram because I was late. I would have preferred to travel without Tanja. She wouldn’t be able to **give** me such **a grilling** once we were at school. And it was clear that she didn’t want to wait any longer to hear all the details about yesterday afternoon.

She got on at the third tram stop. She was **tremendously** curious. “What did you wear?” she greeted me. “And what’s going to happen next?”

I wrapped the scarf tighter around my neck and

---

lovesickness – Liebeskummer; flatly – matt;
to give sb a grilling – jmd. ausquetschen; tremendously – hier: wahnsinnig

whispered: "I think I've caught a cold. I can hardly get a word out. I'll tell you all about it tomorrow."

Tanja looked rather **disappointed**, but there was nothing you could do about me losing my voice. We travelled to school in silence.

Pretending to lose my voice was a brilliant **move**. Firstly, I couldn't talk to Tanja, and secondly I was going to tell them at home how cold it had been in Caberg's study. Maybe I wouldn't have to go to the next lesson. Thirdly, only being able to talk in a whisper meant that I had a relatively quiet morning at school, because every teacher nodded sympathetically when I pointed towards my throat with a pitiful expression on my face.

"This winter is particularly bad for colds," said our biology teacher, and off he went on his favourite subject again: **toughen-up**, toughen-up, he couldn't say it often enough.

I couldn't wait to see how Caberg would react towards me. She would probably allow me a few weeks until the extra lessons with her Dietmar started to take effect, I thought as she checked our homework. But I was wrong. I was the second one to be called in front of the class at the blackboard. I took a deep breath and stood up to go to the front.

"Henri has completely lost her voice," Tanja said in an attempt to save me, "she can't get a word out."

---

disappointed – enttäuscht; move – Schachzug;
to toughen-up – abhärten

Caberg looked irritated. "Henriette is not supposed to be singing arias here; she only has to give me the solutions to problems number 4 to 6 from yesterday's homework, do you understand?"

Dietmar had shown me how to do it, but I had probably nodded the whole time, and had not understood anything, of course. How was I supposed to? I had been thinking of Tom all the time, and how right Tanja had been with her horoscope. There was nothing left of Dietmar's explanations. Since yesterday's lesson, I really did feel that I didn't understand a thing about maths anymore. And so I stood at the blackboard, looking **appropriately** blank.

Caberg walked over to the window, looked into the **snow drifts** and tapped the window sill nervously with her middle finger.

Improvising as far as possible, I half managed to solve the problem. Two weeks ago Caberg would probably have given me a D minus for such a performance, but now things were a bit different.

"Well, you've got the right **approach**, Henriette," she said, as amiably as possible. "I won't be **marking** it today. It's nearly Christmas, after all."

The next few days were completely non-eventful. I walked around with a thick scarf wrapped around my neck all the time, and everyone believed that I had a terrible cold.

---

appropriately – dementsprechend; snow drifts – Schneetreiben; approach – Ansatz; to mark – benoten

"You look terribly ill," determined Babette, who had come home for the weekend. "You can tell from your eyes, especially. They are really swollen."

Was it any wonder? I cried over Tom probably for two hours every day, **mourning** my dilemma, and getting annoyed about my own stupidity, about Tanja, Dietmar Caberg, school and everything else in general. Thank heavens it was soon time for the Christmas holidays. That would give a chance for **dust to settle** a bit **on** the matter of extra tuition. But first of all I had to try to get out of the next lesson with Dietmar.

"I think I can't go to extra tuition today," I **croaked** early on Tuesday morning. "School is about the most I can manage today."

Dad wanted to nod sympathetically, but Mum reckoned that a bit of **change** would do me good. For the last few days, I had been spending the afternoons just sitting around in my bedroom. We'd have to pay for the lesson, anyway, unless we cancelled no later than the evening before. End of subject.

Dad smiled at me, as if to say "**Chin up**". He could laugh. He didn't have to spend afternoons together with Dietmar in a stinky old junk room. I ignored his attempts to cheer me up, and put on the iciest expression I could.

---

to mourn – betrauern; the dust settles on sth – über etwas wächst Gras; to croak – krächzen; change – hier: Abwechslung; chin up – Kopf hoch

A change, that's what my mother had said. I would rather tidy up my room a whole afternoon for a change than spend it with curly Dietmar in his study. For a moment I played with the idea of not going to Luisenstraße at all, and visiting Tanja instead. Then I remembered that we were not the best of friends at the moment. Anyway, Caberg would certainly ring up in the evening, and then I'd have to give a lengthy explanation to my parents. No, I would have to swallow the bitter pill. Another nine lessons with Dietmar and then never again, I told myself and stomped off like Rumpelstiltskin.

It was no effort to get ready for my meeting with Dietmar. I just put on my oldest pair of jeans, the ones with the grass stains on the knee, together with a **sloppy** grey woollen jumper that used to belong to my sisters. When I was under the shower that morning I automatically made a grab for the shampoo because my hair always looked very **drab** and greasy after two days at the most. But since it was a Dietmar-day, I decided to go another day without washing my hair.

"Grey mouse goes to visit Dietmar curly locks," I said to my reflection, poking my tongue out at myself before I left the house. At least I wouldn't freeze in this jumper.

I hadn't cried for about twenty hours now, and not thought about Tom for forty minutes. Lately, when-

---

sloppy – schlabbrig; drab – trostlos

ever I saw someone who showed only the slightest **resemblance** to him, my heart had almost stopped beating, but now nearly three quarters of an hour had passed without me giving him a single thought. There was hope that I would soon get over my great love. I might turn out to be like my sisters, **callous** and cold. But then again I couldn't spend the rest of my life mourning after Tom. And how was I so certain that Tom really was his name? Maybe Tanja had imagined it all. I'd come to expect anything of her lately. Maybe he was called Rüdiger or Alfons or Alois. *Rüdiger-Alois and Henriette Schneider are pleased to announce their engagement.* I giggled. It was best to stay single. At least that way you don't have any trouble with men.

The only stupid thing was that Tanja still believed that **it was** all still **on** with Tom. Yesterday at break time she had invited me to her birthday party in February. "Are you going to bring Tom with you?" she wanted to know.

Christiane and Evelyn heard that, of course.

"Who's this Tom then?" Evelyn wanted to know immediately, and narrowed her eyes.

She thinks she's irresistible like that, Tanja reckons. I tend to think that she's short-sighted. She's probably wondering whether she could **pinch** Tom **off** me.

---

resemblance – Ähnlichkeit; callous – herzlos;
sth is on – eine Sache läuft; to pinch off – ausspannen

"Go on, do tell us!" Christiane demanded and looked at me curiously. "Have you got a boyfriend then, or is it your little brother?"

"No, it's her rich uncle from the old people's home," declared Tanja.

"And he's definitely coming?" Evelyn straightened her jumper, and still seemed to be most interested.

She really does make you sick at times. I nodded to Tanja and whispered that Tom couldn't wait to see her. But he didn't have much time at the moment, unfortunately. I couldn't think of a good reason why, so I just **pretended** to have a huge coughing fit.

I would have felt much better if I'd told Tanja everything. All this pretending was getting on my nerves. After the holidays were over I would tell her that I'd split up with Tom, I thought. But for what reason? Tom has found another girl. That's stupid! Tom is moving to another town. I can't say that because, officially, he is supposed to be Caberg's son.

It was **maddening**. I decided to wait until the new year to solve this problem, and to concentrate on my maths extra tuition instead.

The door to the flat on the fourth floor of Luisenstraße was slightly **ajar**. I coughed slightly and Caberg appeared in front of me, wearing a red and green checked apron. She had **dough** sticking to her fingers. "Go on in! He'll be there in a minute. You

---

to pretend – vortäuschen; maddening – zum Verrücktwerden; ajar – angelehnt; dough – Teig

know where to go." She nodded her head towards the study. The hallway was decorated in the spirit of Christmas with bits of **fir-tree** and brightly-coloured flashing lights.

I heard a **clatter** coming out of the kitchen. Was little Dietmar being allowed to lick the bowl, maybe? I pulled the zip of my anorak right up to the top, and walked towards the study. There had been a change in the weather over the last few days. It had become warmer, and I had felt really hot on the tram. But in this **cold chamber**, called the study, I would even keep my gloves on. If necessary, I could even pull my scarf over my head in case my ears got too cold.

But as soon as I opened the door, I could tell that something was not right. The study, which the last time had been a bit like a foretaste for a trip to the north pole, was now **stifling** hot. It nearly took my breath away. Forty degrees Celcius at least, I estimated. Immediately I pulled off my gloves, anorak and scarf, and rushed to the window. But the **handle** on the window had been removed. Was Caberg afraid that one of the pupils would jump from the fourth floor out of sheer desperation with curly Dietmar?

"It was a bit **chilly** in this room last time," said Caberg who was standing next to her son at the door watching me. "That's where you caught your cold, isn't it?"

---

fir-tree – Tannenbaum; clatter – Klappern;
cold chamber – Kältekammer; stifling – drückend;
handle – Griff; chilly – kühl

I could only nod. After five minutes in this room my throat had all dried up. "Could we perhaps open the window a bit?" I whispered.

Dr Caberg shook her head regretfully. "A little **niece** of mine came to visit me yesterday. Four years old, a really wild little thing. We had to remove the handles from all the windows because she wanted to sit on the **windowsill** all the time. From the outside!" She shook her head in bewilderment. "The ideas children get. And then little Alice got so furious that she hid all the handles. We still haven't found them yet, unfortunately."

If you or your funny Dietmar had a talent for **handling** kids, then I might not be sitting in an oven here now, I thought to myself but didn't say anything. Besides, I seemed to be the only one sweating. No wonder, with this thick jumper. Babette had got it for a skiing trip in the Bavarian Forest, where it is known to be so cold that even wolves live there. I felt how the first beads of sweat gathered on my forehead. I would have liked to have torn off my jumper, but I remembered just in time that I was only wearing a thin **vest** underneath. Dietmar would probably faint. And how Caberg would stare!

That lesson was a complete waste of money, just like the previous one. My poor parents were paying in the belief that I was learning something here. But

---

niece – Nichte; windowsill – Fensterbrett;
to handle – umgehen mit, handhaben; vest – Unterhemd

I only understood about half of what Dietmar was **reeling off** in his quiet voice.

"Have you understood?" he asked me for the fifth time at least, and for the fifth time at least I nodded wordlessly.

Caberg placed a plate of home-made Christmas biscuits on the table for us. "Henriette, try the **cinnamon stars**. Dietmar made those."

She gave me a searching look. Had she noticed the beads of sweat that were slowly running down my **hairline**?

"I'll get you something to drink," she offered.

"Could you switch off the heating, please?" I croaked. I was feeling dizzy by now, and the very thought of Dietmar's home-made cinnamon biscuits made my stomach turn over. I wouldn't be able to stand it much longer in this oven.

Dr Caberg felt the radiator. "It's only luke-warm'.

She placed her hand on my forehead. "Let me feel. Oh dear!" she said. "I think you've got a temperature. Not the **flu**, I hope! Dietmar, go and take three vitamin tablets quickly and go into the living room. I don't want you to catch anything."

Dietmar got up in a hurry, covering his mouth and nose with his hand, and disappeared, probably to gulp down some vitamin tablets as quickly as possible, just like his mother had instructed.

Meanwhile, Dr Caberg had packed all my things

---

to reel off – herunterleiern; cinnamon star – Zimtstern; hairline – Haaransatz; flu – Grippe

together, and said that she would not be charging anything for the lesson, of course, or only half the amount at the most. She also wrapped up Dietmar's cinnamon stars for me. That was rather kind of her, I thought, until it occurred to me that she probably just wanted to get rid of me as fast as possible, before I started spreading any more **germs**. But never mind; it was still better than having to spend another quarter of an hour listening to Dietmar's **soporific** voice, then go home on the tram, followed by a ten minutes' walk.

Dietmar called after me from the living room, saying that I should repeat pages thirty-eight to sixty-four in the maths book.

"Yes, do a bit of revision during the Christmas holidays," said Caberg encouragingly, as we went down the stairs.

I clung tightly to the **banister** because I was feeling dizzy again.

"You're as white as a sheet," determined Caberg, and grabbed me by the arm. All I wanted to do was to lie down on the next **half-landing** and close my eyes.

There were two rings at the doorbell downstairs. Caberg looked at her watch in surprise. "It's only five past three," she established.

Meanwhile, Dietmar had pressed the door opener, and someone was hurrying up the stairs taking long strides.

---

germs – Bazillen; soporific – einschläfernd;
banister – Geländer; half-landing – Treppenabsatz

“Tom, you’re too early, your lesson doesn’t begin until quarter to four,” I heard Dr Caberg say far off in the distance.

I clenched at the banister. Tom? Of course Tom! Not Tom Caberg but Tom whatever his name, one of Dietmar’s pupils for extra tuition. Why hadn’t I thought of that right away? Life was **marvellous**, life was simply wonderful.

Tom was standing in front of me and was looking straight into my eyes. “Hello,” he said and smiled at me.

Then Dietmar called from upstairs to say that he could already come up. They would then just finish earlier.

“Henriette, are you feeling that bad?” she asked concerned.

I sat on the stairs and grinned at her. I had just seen Tom, and I still found he was as nice as on the last two occasions. Or I had I just seen a **mirage**? Was I dreaming? After all, you do see ghosts sometimes when you’re **delirious**.

“Was that just …?” I asked.

“Tom? Yes, I don’t know why he’s here so early today.” Shaking her head, she helped me up, **bundled** me into her car and drove me home.

“I think Henriette’s condition is very serious,” she said to my mother who was standing at the door, looking alarmed. “She was singing all the way here.”

---

marvellous – herrlich; mirage – Fata Morgana;
delirious – im Fieberwahn; to bundle – stopfen, packen

Life was simply worth living. It was **sleeting** outside, the sky was grey and cloudy, and I was lying in bed with a temperature of 40 degrees Celsius. But I was happy. Breakfast was brought to me in bed – with an egg, although it wasn't even Sunday. Nobody grumbled when I spilled the cocoa. Dad even brought me a sports magazine from the kiosk, and placed the telephone next to my bed. "If you should feel any worse, ring us up immediately," he **impressed upon** me. "Anette is coming at about twelve o'clock and she can look after you."

Nobody had to look after me. In fact, all I wanted was to be left alone so that I could think about my **encounter** on the staircase all the time. It had been **fate**, of course, that Tom had come too early on that very day. If I hadn't become ill, I would have sat through the rest of the lesson, and Tom might have had to wait in the living room, and never would we

---

it's sleeting – es fällt Eisregen; to impress upon sb – jmd. einschärfen; encounter – Begegnung; fate – Schicksal

have met. I started to feel funny at the very thought. But, fortunately, that's not what had happened. Tom had smiled at me so nicely. Had he remembered the time when we gazed into each other's eyes that evening at the check-out in the supermarket? There wasn't the slightest doubt: I was in love with him more than ever. And suddenly, the chance of getting to know him had become realistic again.

"Henriette Schneider, you **saved** three **penalties** when you were reserve goalie. Surely you can manage to catch Tom," I said to myself, and had to laugh.

I had to manage it by Tanja's birthday party. **What a nuisance** that the holidays were coming up, and that there wouldn't be any extra tuition.

I'd worked it out: there were twenty days to go until the next lesson. I had to hold out until then. I would cleverly ask Dietmar for all the important information, and then I'd have to wait and see.

There were only three days to go until Christmas, and I was still in bed and didn't have any proper presents. I could hardly wrap up the half empty perfume bottle for Mum, and I just didn't dare to fill it up with clear water. Perhaps Tanja had a good idea! I rang her up at about half-past one in the afternoon. She sounded terribly sleepy when she answered.

"It was so **dreary** today," she mumbled. "Christmas

---

to save a penalty – einen Elfmeter halten;
what a nuisance – wie ärgerlich; dreary – öde

party, headmaster's speech, well, you know, all that rubbish. I'm gradually getting bored with hearing the word Christmas. Be glad that you've been ill so often lately. I've already thought about going into **hibernation**." She giggled. "By the way, I was watching a film until half-past midnight last night with Ronald in the lead role. Hey, he's just absolutely fantastic, I can tell you." By now her voice was sounding very much more wide awake.

"Yeah," I said, "how nice. What are you getting for Christmas this year?"

"What? For you?" Tanja asked astonished.

"No, I mean your family, of course," I said hastily.

Please don't let Tanja have a present for me, otherwise I'll have to buy her something, too, and I didn't even know what to put under the Christmas tree for my parents and sisters on Christmas Eve.

"We've just agreed to give each other something small," Tanja told me, "we don't want to get involved in all that consumerism any more. My mother is buying me a silver-metallic anorak, I'm getting money for a stereo set from my father, a pair of **flared trousers** from his new girlfriend, a ticket from my brother for a concert of …"

I interrupted her. "No, I actually wanted to know what you're buying. Perhaps you can give me an idea."

Tanja laughed. "Shall I bring a magazine around?

---

hibernation – Winterschlaf; flared trousers – Schlaghosen

'A thousand gift ideas in a price range from three to three hundred euros!' You're bound to find something there. I'll read some of it out to you. How about a shower gel stand in the shape of Mickey Mouse for your sister? I've ordered something similar for my brother: a toothbrush and holder in a Ferrari stand. I'm sure Simon will be thrilled with that. Or what d'you think about a white-lace apron for your Mum? Looks **dead posh** and it only costs 14.99. Henri, are you still there? You're not saying anything."

Somehow I felt that these suggestions for presents would not help me much. I thanked Tanja for her help, promised to get in touch with her as soon as I was feeling better, and put the receiver down in frustration.

I could vividly imagine what Christmas Eve would be like. We, too, had all agreed to give each other only small presents, but it wouldn't be any different than with Tanja. My sisters and mother had certainly bought expensive presents for me. They would all be **generous**; it was only me that didn't have anything for them. And they would all say: "But it doesn't really matter, Henri is the youngest and doesn't have to give us anything." A **disgrace**, a terrible disgrace. I had to think of something.

I worked out roughly how much pocket money I

---

dead posh – todschick, piekfein; generous – großzügig; disgrace – Blamage

still had, and came to a lousy eleven euros. To buy presents for Mum, Dad, Babette, Anette and possibly Robert as well, would mean just about two euros per person. Then rather no presents at all. Five years ago I could make my parents happy with pictures painted by myself. I mass-produced Father Christmases standing in front of the Christmas tree, and nobody seemed to notice that I gave the same picture away several times, first of all to my grandparents, and then when they'd left, to my aunties, and then finally Anette received one for her birthday on 28th December.

Precisely, that was the very idea! I pulled on two jumpers, one on top of the other, and ran down into the cellar. After half an hour I had found what I was looking for. Probably out of sheer sentimentality, Mum had kept the scarf with the **rosebud pattern** that I had printed when I was in the 4th year at primary school. No-one would remember that I had already given her this precious garment for Mother's Day years ago, and even if they did, they wouldn't dare say a thing on Christmas Eve. At least, that's what I hoped. I wrapped the scarf in dark blue paper, wrote *For Mum – from Henriette,* using a gold pen, and felt quite satisfied. That's what you call recycling.

Unfortunately, I couldn't do the same thing for Dad. Because I usually give him sweets, it was only

---

rosebud pattern – Rosenmuster

logical that there was nothing left of them. So I would have to give him a **voucher** again, and hope that he would forget to **redeem** it. "3 x breakfast in bed, 3 x cleaning shoes, 3 x vacuuming the car," I wrote in my best handwriting on a sheet of hand-crafted writing paper that I had pinched from him. That was plenty enough, I thought; after all, we only wanted to give each other something small. That just left my dear sisters. I realized that I couldn't just give them vouchers.

A day before Christmas Eve I had found the solution. I bought two telephone cards from my Dad, wrapped them up elaborately, and tied a pink marzipan pig onto each parcel. My sisters could think what they wanted of that. Anyway, I had my presents, and could look forward to Christmas.

Christmas itself was rather uneventful, disregarding the fact that Anette and Robert were talking about getting engaged on Christmas Day, and that by **Boxing Day**, Anette had decided to leave him, this time definitely, as she kept repeating. She brought all of her stuff home, and took over her room and part of the living room. When I used her shower gel by mistake, she complained half the morning, and reproached me for the twenty-fifth time that I had taken her new mohair jumper out of her wardrobe without permission, had worn it before her, and to

---

voucher – Gutschein; to redeem – einlösen;
Boxing Day – 26. Dezember

crown it all, had poured some revolting perfume all over it. She took her bad mood out on the entire family. But apart from that, and the fact that I had to keep thinking of Tom, there was a really festive atmosphere in our home. Perhaps that got on Anette's nerves because on New Year's Day she moved back into Robert's apartment.

In the general chaos of those days, it was hardly noticed when we were exchanging presents that I gave Mum the scarf with the roses. I was hoping that her memory wasn't too good. She was a bit confused, though, when she unpacked it: "Lovely, Henriette. You made it yourself, didn't you?"

Anette mumbled something like "**looks** a bit **familiar to me**," but at that moment I unpacked the present from my grandparents, and suddenly everyone was quiet.

"Perhaps it's her age," said Dad uncertainly, when he saw what I was holding in my hand. "I mean, Grandma is nearly eighty, after all, and so much knitting can certainly turn you crazy."

"Perhaps the other one is for me or Anette," Babette suggested, and was going to take one of the two long woollen scarves from my hand. I looked at her indignantly. "Your parcel is back there, and Anette has already unpacked her socks," I said. I was determined to defend the two brightly striped scarves – one for me and one for Tom – to the bitter end.

---

looks familiar to me – kommt mir bekannt vor

"Or maybe Grandma knitted it for one of the neighbour's children, and packed it up by mistake," guessed my mother.

"But it says here in extra large letters 'For Henri'" I said, and smoothed out the crumpled Christmas wrapping paper. "I assume that Grandma knows how many scarves and gloves I have already lost, and that's why she is sending me a spare one at the same time."

My parents nodded. This argument **made sense** to them. I quickly **rescued** my two scarves, and planned to ring up Grandma the very next day to thank her for my present and to ask her not to say anything about my strange request ("two identical scarves") to anyone. We then went on unpacking our presents.

Towards the end of the holidays I visited Tanja again after a long time. She had rung me several times to ask me whether I had any time. I replied **evasively** a few times, and Tanja promptly suspected that it had something to do with Tom. But then on the last Friday before school started, I did go to visit her.

"Well? Do you notice anything?" she asked proudly, when I turned up at about half-past two, absolutely frozen.

"Yeah, it's freezing cold," I said.

Tanja pulled me nearer to the window. "About

---

to make sense – einleuchten, vernünftig klingen;
to rescue – retten; evasively – ausweichend

me, I mean. Do you notice anything different about me?"

Yes, it was true, Tanja had changed. A small **gem** was glittering on her right nostril.

"What do you think of it?"

I nodded **in approval**. "Doesn't it hurt?"

Tanja pulled a face. "You sound just like my grandmother. No, of course it doesn't hurt, at least, not that much. And have a look at this. That's what my father gave me." She fetched a gold and silver-coloured bag out of the wardrobe. "And the best thing is to come. I've got an autograph from Ronald Reimann. With a **dedication**!" Almost tenderly she removed the photograph in the gold frame from her bedside table, and held it out to me. "For Tanja from Ronald Reimann" was written in large letters diagonally across the photograph of a blond man with a three-day beard.

"I'm just so incredibly happy." She pressed the picture against her body and smiled. "And now tell me all about you and Tom."

"Oh, there's not all that much to tell," I **claimed**, feeling rather uncomfortable. "In fact, there's nothing new at all at the moment. How on earth did you get Ronald Reimann's autograph?"

Tanja gently returned the picture to the bedside table, straightened her glasses and looked at me mys-

---

gem – Edelstein; in approval – anerkennend;
dedication – Widmung; to claim – behaupten

teriously. "You won't believe it, but I dreamed that Ronald was here in our town. I kept having the same dream for three nights. It was driving me completely mad, and in the end I told my mother about it. Because she knows all about stars and horoscopes and all that. Well, I told my mother all about the dream, and then she just looked at me and said, well of course, it's all true; Ronald Reimann has been staying at the 'Golden Angel' for three days. She'd even seen him twice. – Oh, Henri, was I pleased that my mother works there. She managed to get me his autograph on the very same evening. Actually, I wanted to talk to him myself, but my mother didn't want that, but all the same, I've now got his autograph with a personal dedication."

Tanja had completely forgotten the subject of Tom. For the rest of the afternoon we thought about whether it would be possible to make a trip to Berlin during the next summer holidays, as in the meantime Tanja had found out Ronald's address there.

"Perhaps we could go with my brother," Tanja considered. "Then the journey won't cost us anything, and we'll just stay in a **youth hostel** in Berlin. Why don't you ask your parents straight away?"

I was feeling guilty about fibbing so much about Tom. So I **solemnly** promised to get down on my hands and knees that very weekend, and beg my par-

---

youth hostel – Jugendherberge; solemnly – feierlich

ents to let me go to Berlin with Tanja in the summer holidays.

"You're a real friend," said Tanja, "I'll never forget this. And if you ever need help with Tom, you can count on me any time."

Of course I need help, I thought when I was sitting in front of the television that evening, watching the thirty-second episode of "Heidhoferstraße, 4th floor" starring Ronald Reimann. All the optimism I had after the encounter on the stairs had **evaporated**. To accidentally meet Tom at the Cabergs was not quite as easy as I had imagined in my daydreams. Maybe that had been his last lesson with Dietmar, which was why he had come too early because he was so happy that he didn't have to go there any more.

I could still **crawl to** Dietmar and squeeze some information out of him about his other pupil. My next appointment at Luisenstraße was in four days, and then I would know more.

I gathered my thoughts together and tried to concentrate on Ronald Reimann, who had just prevented a young woman from jumping out of the window by smiling at her and telling her that she was still needed. The end credits music had just started when the telephone began to ring.

It was Tanja.

---

to evaporate – sich verflüchtigen;
to crawl to sb – sich bei jmd. einschleimen

Her first question, of course, was whether I had just seen Roland, and I was able to say yes with an **easy conscience**.

"I'm up for Berlin," she **babbled on** immediately. "But my mother would prefer it if there were the two of us. Berlin is a large city after all and …"

"I haven't asked yet," I said **in an undertone**, "my parents are just coming. I'll just ask them now."

"What are you just going to ask now?" yelled Dad, who was just hanging up his warm winter coat on the **hallstand**.

It's funny, sometimes you have to tell him something three times over, and other times he has very sharp ears all of a sudden. "What does our daughter want this time?" he asked.

Mum threw him a meaningful glance, as if to say: leave her alone! Just be thankful that she's back to normal again, more or less, and not **moping around** here every afternoon, crying all the time like just before Christmas.

"I've got to go now," I said to Tanja. "We're having supper."

I had just sat down at the dining table when the telephone started ringing again.

"Henri, you answer it," yelled Dad from the bathroom. "It'll be for you, anyway."

"Well? Can you come?" Tanja wanted to know.

---

easy conscience – gutes Gewissen; to babble on – losplappern; in an undertone – halblaut; hallstand – Flurgarderobe; moping around – trübsinnig herumhängen

“Things don’t move quite that fast here. I’ll ring you up, either today or tomorrow,” I promised her.

“Wait a minute, don’t hang up yet,” Tanja shouted into the receiver, “my brother might also be staying in Berlin for a few days. At least there will be an adult with us then. Simon is nineteen, after all. Tell your parents that, and that will **ease their minds**.”

I had my doubts whether Simon’s presence in Berlin would persuade my parents, but I couldn’t tell Tanja that, of course. So I mumbled something like “Right-o, will do, talk to you soon,” and put the receiver down.

“Might that have been your bosom friend Tanja, by any chance?” inquired Dad as I sat back down at the table.

I fished out a **gherkin** and nodded.

“Say, what about your friends from the football club, why don’t they get in touch any more?” my mother wondered. “Don’t you do any training in the winter?”

You can never please your parents. They’ve been giving me trouble about training for the last three years. “Football is much too hard a sport for girls,” Mum says regularly, and starts **dishing out** pearls of wisdom from the last century. I was given vouchers for ballet lessons and trial riding lessons, but all my parents’ efforts were in vain. I had football training twice a week. That is until I started having extra

---

to ease sb’s mind – jmd. beruhigen; gherkin – Gewürzgurke; to dish out sth – etwas zum Besten geben, auftischen

tuition in maths. And now, all of a sudden, I was supposed to justify why I don't go to training any more. It's impossible to understand parents sometimes.

"Our team hasn't got any chance of promotion at the moment. Too many were ill over the last three months." I looked deep into Mum's eyes. "You've got no idea how much training is necessary to put up a half-decent team. If I were to stop extra tuition, and go to four training sessions instead ..."

"Don't you dare, don't you dare!" Mum raised her hands in defence. "**That'll be the limit**. You'll end up having to repeat the class, and all because of playing football."

I couldn't help grinning. "Well there you are then! It's much more sensible to miss a few training sessions every now and again, and do something for school instead."

That was clearly one point **in my favour**. I didn't have to tell my parents that in the meantime I had come to regard my footballer's legs as a great obstacle in competition with other girls. A little less training, and the problem would solve itself, I had thought to myself, and simply missed the last two sessions.

"What did Tanja want just now?" inquired Dad again.

I placed two slices of cheese and a gherkin on my

---

that'll be the limit – so weit kommt's noch;
in favour – zu Gunsten

bread, and took a bite first. I needed time to think. Perhaps Berlin wasn't such a bad idea. It's true, I didn't feel in the least bit like hanging around Ronald Reimann's house all day, waiting for him to appear, but on the other hand – perhaps Tom could come along too. At any rate, I didn't want to **drive** my parents **around the bend** with Tanja's plans for Berlin, not straight away.

I swallowed, emptied my cup of tea, and said quite casually: "Tanja is going to Berlin in the summer holidays. On her own, or with her brother. It hasn't been decided yet."

My parents glanced at each other, and you could hear Dad take a breath. "Aha! And why are you telling us all this?"

I was completely baffled. Who had been **pestering** me with questions all the time?

The telephone rang again, and I stood up.

"You didn't by any chance want to ask us whether you could go to Berlin with your friend Tanja in the summer holidays?" inquired Mum.

"Don't worry," I shouted from the hallway when I picked up the receiver, "I'll be coming to Austria with you again."

"Don't say you can't come!" there was an **indignant** cry from the receiver. "Damn, Henri, my mother has just stressed that I can only go if you come with me."

---

to drive sb around the bend – jmd. verrückt machen; to pester – bedrängen; indignant – empört

"Just wait! I can't **nag** my parents about it just yet otherwise they will **clam up** completely. It's a long time until the summer holidays, and who knows what will happen by then," I whispered. That sentence sounded good, I thought, and it had its effect. Tanja calmed down again.

"Oh, and another thing," I added. "Don't ring up again this evening. My father will **go ballistic** otherwise."

"Alright then. We'll talk more about it in school on Monday," she suggested. "My mother can talk to your parents, if necessary."

The first day at school after the Christmas holidays was a **giveaway**. Nearly all the teachers repeated stuff as if we'd lost our memories with the turn of the year. The only thing of any interest were the conversations during main break in the school yard. Evelyn was talking about her search for an engagement ring.

"Well? Have you got one now?" Tanja asked.

Evelyn pulled a face. "You can't believe how difficult it is to find an engagement ring that isn't conventional or boring!"

Tanja pulled me away. "I'd like to see the bloke who gets engaged to Evelyn voluntarily," she scoffed. "She's just bragging about her fiancé. But I haven't learned a thing about you and Tom. I find that a bit

---

to nag – nerven; to clam up – dichtmachen; to go ballistic – ausflippen; to give away – verschenken

strange. We're friends, after all." She looked at me **sullenly**. "Have you got any secrets from me?"

"'Nooo, of course not," I assured her, and started to think quickly. I simply had to get Tanja off this sensitive subject. Berlin! Precisely. She would jump at that. " What have you got in mind exactly for Berlin?" I asked.

But the change of subject was too sudden. Tanja had become suspicious. "You keep avoiding the subject whenever I start talking about Tom," she said. "I don't even know which school he goes to."

My dear Tanja, that's what I'd like to know as well, I thought, and searched desperately for an excuse. "Yes, well, what is there to say?" I said. "We talk to each other on the phone a lot, and Tom just doesn't have much time."

"Why?" Tanja was not to be satisfied so easily.

I was fibbing again, I realized in horror. Why did Tom have so little time, actually? My eyes fell on the "Young Musicians" poster, and I suddenly knew why.

"I'll tell you a secret," I whispered, and took Tanja aside. "Tom is not only an excellent mathematician, but he also plays the violin brilliantly. He will be taking part in a **competition** soon. That's why he hasn't got much time for me at the moment."

That **made an impact**. Tanja looked at me in **awe**. "Will he be giving a concert sometime?"

---

sullenly – missmutig; competition – hier: Wettbewerb;
to make an impact – Eindruck machen; awe – Ehrfurcht

I frowned. "I don't know, he might do. But Tanja, it's an absolute state secret. Caberg doesn't want anyone to know about it under any circumstances. You'll keep quiet, won't you?!"

Tanja took my hand, shook it three times, and promised not to tell a soul. "Although," she said after thinking for a short while, "Caberg can be really proud of her Tom. It wouldn't be so terrible if our class knew that …"

"Don't you dare," I shouted at her. "That would cause a whole lot of problems because …" I caught myself biting my fingernails. One lie led to the next one, I realized again.

"Yes, because?" Tanja asked curiously. It was obvious that she wasn't going to be shaken off today. I looked around, searching for help.

Dr Caberg, who was just on **yard duty**, discovered me at that very moment, and waved at me. I would normally ignore this kind of thing, but now I literally rushed up to her.

"Well, did you have a good holiday? And have you done any revision?"

"Of course," I declared. I had a good holiday, at least.

"That's good. I wanted to ask if you could come for your lesson this afternoon, just this once. Dietmar's got an appointment at the dentist's tomorrow and we …"

---

yard duty – Pausenaufsicht

I thought as quick as a flash and then nodded. "No problem." The sooner I found out something about Tom the better.

Unfortunately, Dietmar behaved as though he'd **signed the secrecy act**. I did a fair bit of crawling, and insisted that I was once again enjoying maths since I'd started having lessons with him, and then asked, ever so innocently, up to what level does he teach? But curly Dietmar simply ignored my question. "I think it's great that you're already giving extra tuition at your age," and then added, "how old are you, anyway?"

That question could only be answered with a **figure**, and I was sure that's what he would do. "Sixteen," Dietmar replied promptly, "I'm sixteen."

I bet Tom isn't any older than that, I thought, because even a **whizz kid** like Dietmar wouldn't be giving tuition to someone from the upper school. Perhaps I should just ask him directly: "Can you tell me what Tom's **surname** is, and where does he live? And does he have a girlfriend, or not? And does he mind girls with footballer's legs?" I did no such thing, of course, but behaved myself and continued solving the problems on a piece of **rough paper** that Dietmar kept passing to me as if we were on an **assembly line**.

---

to sign the secrecy act – einen Verschwiegenheitseid leisten; figure – Zahl; whizz kid – Wunderkind, Genie; surname – Familienname; rough paper – Schmierpapier; assembly line – Fließband

Shortly before the end of the lesson, the doorbell rang.

Would that be Tom? I could feel how I turned pale from excitement. Of course, it could only be Tom. Hadn't Caberg said that morning in the school yard that the appointments for Tuesday had to be cancelled? I **wriggled about** on my chair.

Dietmar looked at me with a frown. "What's the matter with you? Have you got to go to the toilet?"

"The doorbell rang," I said **hoarsely**. My God, I was nervous.

"So what? Look here, you can solve problem number eight much easier like this if you …"

The doorbell was now ringing for the third time.

"Mammy," yelled Dietmar, "can you open the door, please!"

"Can't. I'm just in the bath," we heard Dr Caberg's muffled voice coming from the bathroom. "You go and see to it!"

I would like to have jumped up and pressed the door opener.

Dietmar got up slowly, and trotted to the door. "Go on with the problems," he said to me, "we've still got precisely eight minutes."

Of course, I had more important things to do than maths. When Dietmar grabbed the receiver of the intercom, I held my breath.

---

to wriggle about – hin und her rutschen; hoarsely – heiser

"It's only the **chimney sweep**," he shouted to his mother.

The chimney sweep! I noticed how I slumped back in my chair. All the excitement was for nothing. But chimney sweeps are supposed to bring loads of luck. I had to seize the opportunity while Dietmar wasn't in the room.

With a swift movement of my hand, I grabbed his exercise book and flicked through the pages. All the problems from my maths book had been neatly stuck into it, with all the answers underneath. Teacher's manual, I concluded with incredible logic, and grinned. On the first page in large print stood: *Extra tuition Henriette S., 8th form.* Dietmar had probably heard something about the **protection of personal data**. "Henriette S." – that sounded quite ridiculous. Disappointed, I put the book back, and a small yellow note fluttered out. Dietmar's timetable for extra tuition. *Tuesday, half-past two Henriette S.,* I read. Right, I knew that myself. But then it became interesting. *Quarter to four, Tom D.* And exactly the same on Thursday. And there was nothing to indicate that this timetable was no longer **applicable**.

On Thursday it would happen. This time I was absolutely sure.

I carefully pushed the note back, and leaned over my notes.

---

chimney sweep – Kaminkehrer; protection of personal data – Datenschutz; applicable – anwendbar, gültig

The time was actually up, but I knew Dietmar by now. “We’ve still got exactly eight minutes,” he said when he returned to the study. “Or would you rather come eight minutes earlier next time?”

This time

it was going to happen, definitely. I was best prepared, my hair had been freshly washed and I had put on a new jumper (my own one, this time). I'd come across Grandma's Christmas scarf, and I decided to wrap it around my neck as a talisman. Satisfied, I checked myself in the mirror. Compared with Evelyn I still looked rather **plain**, and I couldn't match the gem in Tanja's nose. I looked around, undecided. Should I borrow something from Mum, a **brooch** maybe, and stick it on my scarf? No, that won't do, I decided. And then I had a brilliant idea. I took the second scarf that was actually intended for Tom, and wound that around my neck as well. That looked a bit cheerful and **jaunty**, I thought. That's how I would go to school tomorrow. I smiled at my reflection, grabbed my little rucksack that I had packed with special care that day, and ran off to be at Dr Caberg's study at half-past two, punctual as ever.

---

plain – unscheinbar; brooch – Brosche; jaunty – flott

"My mother has gone shopping," curly Dietmar greeted me at the door. He didn't have a **side parting** any more, but had combed his hair off his forehead. "But you can still come in".

I had to **giggle**. Had Dr Caberg perhaps forbidden her son to let any strangers into the flat in her absence? I sat down at the table in the study and pulled my papers out of the rucksack, which I then kicked **surreptitiously** between the two bookshelves on the long side of the room.

Now I was ready. Dietmar was already explaining the first problems to me. I managed to **suppress** a yawn with effort. I examined the position of the rucksack. With the tip of my toe I pushed it a bit further. It slightly **tilted** over backwards. Now it couldn't be seen at all from where Dietmar was sitting. Brilliant! **There you are**, I knew it; plan number two would work out.

The idea had come to me during the last episode of "Heidhoferstraße, 4th floor", when Ronald Reimann, taking the part of Mike Hardenstein, had deliberately left his mobile phone at a neighbour's on the 4th floor. Around midnight he rang himself up using a false name, and insisted on talking to Mike urgently, and the woman really did march over to him at midnight. The rest was clear. I now had something similar in mind.

---

side parting – Seitenscheitel; to giggle – kichern; surreptitiously – unauffällig; to suppress – unterdrücken; to tilt – kippen; there you are – na bitte!

"Is anything wrong?" asked Dietmar, and looked worried. "Is that too difficult for you? Should I start from the very beginning?"

I shook my head and did my best to follow his intellectual flights. Actually, it wasn't all that difficult; I just wasn't able to concentrate. The next time, I **resolved**, I will pay full attention for forty-five minutes.

At quarter-past three on the dot, the door opened quietly, and Dr Caberg poked her head in. "Hello, Henriette!" she greeted me kindly.

I passed her the envelope with the money, and smiled back.

"You have to finish on time," said Dr Caberg, turning to her son, "you know that Tom ...!"

Did that mean that Tom would be coming earlier today? I gathered up all my courage. "Is Tom coming earlier today?" I asked and looked intensely out of the window into the dark-grey January sky. My voice sounded hoarse and unnatural to me.

But neither Caberg or Dietmar seemed to notice. He wanted to say something, but his mother just said, "No, no," and she reminded me that the next maths test was only **just around the corner**. I was sure that I would move out of the danger zone and do better than an E, I said, thanks to Dietmar's help, and said goodbye quickly. I couldn't stand around for too

---

to resolve – beschließen; to be just around the corner – vor der Tür stehen

long in the study, otherwise one of them might notice that my little rucksack was lying between the two bookshelves.

It all had to look genuine, I had thought. I would go to the tram stop as usual, wait around there for quarter of an hour, then realize with horror that my rucksack was missing, look around a bit, and then run back to the Luisenstraße. Shortly after four I would ring excitedly at Caberg's door, and burst into Tom's lesson. I would just sit and wait on the stairs with my rucksack until he came out. If he had any interest in me at all, then he would say something like: "That must have been an awful shock for you, standing there, without any money or **travel pass**. Shall we go and have a coke together?" I wouldn't say no, and off we would go to a café. Well, yes, that's how I imagined it, at least.

I looked at the clock. Time wasn't passing at all. I still had ages to walk around in this lousy weather. I didn't want to appear too early, under any circumstances. It was just the right time if I …

"Henriette!" someone shouted.

I **gave a start**.

"Henriette!" On the opposite side of the road a woman was getting out of her car and was running towards me. "Quick, here, take your rucksack!" Dr Caberg shouted to me. "It was fortunate that Dietmar saw it. I've got to hurry; I'm in a no-stopping area."

---

travel pass – Monatskarte; to give a start – zusammenzucken

She thrust my small, black rucksack into my hand, and didn't even wait to see if I thanked her for it – which I most certainly wouldn't have done in this particular case – and ran back to her car. When she opened the door, she turned around and shouted to me across the road: "can I **give you a lift** for part of the way?"

I just shook my head. I couldn't think clearly. All that I knew was: everything, but absolutely everything, had gone wrong again. Dietmar, the idiot, probably searched the study after every lesson for any **traces**, probably in the interests of protecting personal data, I suspected. The next time I would stick two chewing gums under the desk. See if his mother would come after me then in her car to bring me the chewing gums. I had to giggle, and at the same time tears came to my eyes.

Why did I always have such bad luck? I wanted to get home as quickly as possible. How embarrassing, crying here at the tram stop in front of everybody. The older woman next to me was already looking at me strangely.

A young woman with lilac hair, wearing a **shabby fur coat** pushed her way though the waiting crowd. "Got a euro for me?" she shouted into the crowd, but most people only looked away.

That's what I would do, normally, saying to myself

---

to give sb a lift – jmd. im Auto mitnehmen; trace – Spur; shabby fur coat – schäbiger Fellmantel

that I'm still at school and only have a bit of pocket-money. But now I began to rummage around my rucksack. Perhaps a miracle might happen with Tom if I gave the woman something, I thought, and for a moment I believed in **fairy tales** again.

But I was catapulted back to reality very quickly. A bunch of keys, pack of chewing gum, school diary, three cough sweets and a comb, that was all I could find in my rucksack. I **futilely** searched the pockets of my anorak and trousers. My purse together with my monthly travel pass for the tram had disappeared.

"Well, are you going to give me a euro?" the lilac-haired woman asked impatiently.

"My purse is gone," I said.

She threw me a **meaningful** look. "That's a new one," she mumbled, and went on.

For a moment, I felt that a miracle had already happened. If I hadn't been going to give the woman some money, I would now be sitting unsuspectingly on the tram, and who knows, an **inspector** might have come along …

I suspected where my purse was lying: in Caberg's study, between the bookshelves. It had slipped out of my rucksack, **presumably**, and had been completely overlooked by Dietmar in his stupidity. I could now burst into Tom's lesson with an easy conscience.

---

fairy tale – Märchen; futilely – vergeblich; meaningful – viel sagend; inspector – hier: Kontrolleur; presumably – vermutlich

You see, everything was nearly going according to plan, even better perhaps.

At the corner of the Sophienstraße and Luisenstraße I started to run. I rang Caberg's doorbell, slightly out of breath. "Dr Caberg," I was going to say, "could you hurry up and open the door, please?"

The important thing was to get into the study. I didn't want to explain down here why I was on her doorstep again. Caberg might otherwise get the idea of looking for the purse herself. I was getting smarter these days. I had come to realize that you have to think of absolutely everything, because in real life, things don't **run** quite as **smoothly** as they do on television.

I rang the bell for the second time, pressing a bit longer this time. Nothing **stirred**. Could it be possible that curly Dietmar's maths lesson was so interesting that they didn't even hear the doorbell? It was more likely that Tom and Dietmar had fallen asleep out of boredom. I pressed the bell a third time. Dietmar and Tom had to be up there alone, since Dr Caberg's car was not in the parking space in front of the house. Why didn't either of them open the door?

I looked around helplessly. On the ground floor I saw a movement behind one of the windows, the curtains were drawn back, and a young woman, with a

---

run smoothly – glatt gehen; to stir – sich rühren

towel wrapped around her head in a turban, opened the window just a **crack**.

"You're the one who always goes to see Caberg, aren't you?" she determined, flicked her cigarette on the pavement, narrowly missing me, and looked at me expectantly.

"Yes, and I just left my purse there with my monthly travel pass," I explained.

"Well, there's nobody there now. Almost exactly half an hour ago," she screwed up her eyes and stared at her watch, "yes, half an hour ago exactly, they both **tramped** down the staircase. Dietmar was complaining to his mother about having to do house visits. His mother hurried him along because she wanted to drop something off at the tram stop, or something like that." The woman lifted her shoulders, **shivering**. "It's getting cold. And I can't help you anyway." She nodded in my direction, and closed the window.

I nodded back, and crawled to the tram stop. I had an addition to make to the Ten Commandments: **Thou** shall not ever make a plan.

But how was I supposed to get home without any money or pass? It was clearly too far on foot.

My mind made up, I got onto the next tram. I might be lucky. Maybe I wouldn't get caught by an inspector. I remained standing although there were

---

crack – Spalt; to tramp – trampeln, stapfen;
to shiver – frösteln; thou – du

some seats vacant. I had never before taken any real notice of the signs strongly advising you against **fare-dodging**. An expensive business!

I looked around me uncertainly. A mother with three children got on, an older woman on crutches and three young men with briefcases. Nobody looked like a ticket inspector. I was about to sit down **in relief** on the next vacant seat, when I saw the man who was just getting up.

He was in his mid forties, brown leather jacket, handbag – an inspector, I bet. The man went to the front. Yep, that's where he would start, and there was probably somebody at the back, too, who was just about to stand up and cut off the way into the open for people like me. We would get to the next stop in half a minute at the latest. If everything went well now, I wouldn't ever lie again in my life, or wear my sister's jumper, or ...

"Next stop Ursulastraße," said the voice from the loudspeaker. I ran to the door.

"Hey, watch out," somebody shouted behind me, and an old man shook his head in annoyance.

I waved in **apology** and rushed off the tram. I would rather walk through the slush for hours than go through a few minutes like that again. I turned around and discovered the man with the little handbag who was hurrying towards me. Was he allowed to

---

fare-dodging – schwarzfahren; in relief – erleichtert; apology – Entschuldigung; slush – Schneematsch

check once we were off the tram? All I wanted to do was run away, but I just didn't have the energy any more.

"It was the only way. My ticket is …," I started to say.

But the man looked at me blankly. "Do you speak English?" he asked. "Can you help me? Where is Sielerstraße?"

I just looked at him with big eyes, and shook my head. I was sorry, but at that moment I didn't understand a word of English, and didn't know where Sielerstraße was, either.

I walked home, tramping through the snow. Apart from me there was hardly anyone else about on foot. The whole of mankind appeared to travelling by bus, tram or car. Damn, I thought, as I started coughing behind a lorry that had just produced a black cloud of diesel, will I be glad when I've got my driving licence. I'll look for a job babysitting or something like that, so that I'll have enough money for a driving licence when I'm 18. Besides, that would distract me from having stupid thoughts about Tom who was now **haunting my head** more than ever.

"You look pretty **shattered**," Anette greeted me, when I eventually arrived home after an eternity.

I only vaguely nodded. What was my sister doing at home again?

---

to haunt sb's head – jmd. im Kopf herumspuken;
shattered – erledigt

"Have you had another argument with Robert?" I asked suspiciously. "Mum will have a **nervous breakdown** if you move back here, you know."

Anette gave me an unfriendly look. "How nice of you to tell me. But don't worry, I'm staying with Robert. You can tell Mum that she can do what she likes with my room. I've only come to pick up a few things." She was obviously annoyed. I was going to say something nice when the doorbell rang.

"Oh dear, I thought Robert wasn't coming until half-past six," exclaimed Anette. "You open the door, I've still got some packing to do."

That was typical of Anette! Just because I'm the youngest, I've always got to do what she says. I didn't feel like talking to her Robert at all. I could well do without his stupid questions today. He behaved like his own grandfather, I thought.

The doorbell rang for the second time. "Come on, Henri, go and answer the door at last! Are you **deaf** or something? You can see that I've got plenty to do," moaned Anette.

I pressed the door opener. It only made sense to do everything just so that Anette and Robert would stay together. Otherwise she would move back in here, and **order me about** all the time. Just this once I decided to greet Robert nicely. With quite a friendly smile on my face I opened the door.

---

nervous breakdown – Nervenzusammenbruch; deaf – taub; to order sb about – jmd. herumkommandieren

"You're Henriette, aren't you?"

Tom! Was I delirious, was it a mirage, or one big hallucination? Tom was standing in front of me, and was holding out my purse to me.

"Yes, I'm Henriette," I said. I couldn't think of anything better. We stood facing each other in silence. His eyes are green, I thought.

"Tell Robert he can start carrying things out," called my sister from her room. "Like the blue suitcase in the hallway, for instance."

Tom **cleared his throat**, and stared at the nameplate on the door. He was still holding my purse in his hand.

"I don't want to hold you up," he said.

"How did you find my purse?" I asked. Everything I said sounded rather **lame**, I thought.

Tom swallowed. "You left your rucksack at the Cabergs', so Mrs Caberg told me. She then brought it to you, but the purse seems to have slipped out. At any rate she found it in her car. And as Dietmar was at my house this afternoon, and I only live a few streets away, I offered to ..." He became silent, uncertain of himself.

"Robert should come and collect the travelling bag," called my sister.

Tom looked slightly confused.

"That's only my sister," I said. "What was Dietmar doing at your house?"

---

to clear one's throat – sich räuspern; lame – lahm

Tom laughed, embarrassed. "Well, because of the extra tuition. My father wanted to listen in on a lesson, and since he's in a wheelchair he can't get to the Cabergs' all that easily, and so Dietmar came to us. A house visit, so to speak."

I nodded, knowingly. "Yes, of course."

"Tell Robert to come and help me at last!" yelled my sister. "In our relationship it's only ever one of us who does all the work. It's ridiculous." She poked her head around the door.

Only then did she notice that it wasn't Robert at the door. "I thought Robert was there," she mumbled. "Typical, you can never **rely on** him." She furiously slammed the door to her room.

In the living room the telephone started ringing.

"I think I'd better go. Bye, then," said Tom when the phone rang for the fourth time, and he thrust the purse into my hand.

I wanted to shout: "No, Tom. Come in, we've got so much to talk about. Do you think Dietmar is such a **nerd**, too? I'm not as strange as my sister. Why are you actually having extra tuition in maths? Can you imagine that I used to be the best at maths in our class? Where do you live? And what's your surname? Do you like football? Do footballer's legs on girls **bother** you?"

---

to rely on sb – sich auf jmd. verlassen; nerd – Blödmann;
to bother – hier: stören

But I simply said "bye," and the front door had already shut.

"Hey, what's the matter with you?" Anette wondered. She pulled me into the hallway. "You've been standing around here for ages, just staring into space. Why didn't you answer the phone? Are you ill?"

I shook my head.

"And where has Robert got to now? Henri, maybe *you* can help me?"

I said that I still had some homework to do, **locked** myself **in** my room, and sat down on the windowsill. The sky was of a dark blue that looked almost unreal. The longer I stared outside, the more stars I discovered.

For a moment I thought I saw a **shooting star**, but then I realized that it was a landing aeroplane. Disappointed, I drew the curtains and lay down on my bed. I was still holding the purse that Tom had brought me.

I'd done it all wrong again. Evelyn would have said: "Hello, Tom, that's really sweet of you to come by especially. Wouldn't you like to come in? I've got a great new CD. Shall we listen to it together?" or something like that at least.

Nobody in my class would have stood around stupidly like I did. Not a single one. I tried to remember what I'd actually said. I'd told him something

---

to lock in – einschließen; shooting star – Sternschnuppe

about my sister, and asked him why Dietmar had been at his house.

It was only because of Anette, I tried to **convince** myself, just because of that silly Anette that I had acted so strangely. Tom must think I'm stupid. If Anette hadn't shouted in the background all the time, I would have behaved in a completely different way. If only, if only, if only!

I started to cry again, also a bit because I knew very well that it wasn't my sister's fault. The problem was with me, and me alone. Whenever I saw Tom, my heart began to race, and I couldn't speak a **sensible** sentence. It had happened at Caberg's that time on the stairs, and again today.

But there was a shimmer of hope. Hadn't Tom said that he'd offered to bring me the purse? How had he known that I only live a few streets away? Caberg is so very careful about discretion.

But perhaps I had misunderstood everything.

It didn't matter. I had missed an opportunity again. This encounter, too, had gone all wrong.

The doorbell rang three times. I got up. Robert had come, and my sister was talking in her **bossy voice** again. I would never talk to Tom like that, I thought. But then again would I ever speak to him again?

---

to convince – überzeugen, einreden; sensible – vernünftig; bossy voice – Befehlston

Forget him. That's what I should do. But it was easier said than done. In the mornings I caught myself looking up and down the people on the tram. Maybe Tom might be on the same tram as me, by some chance. If he only lives a few streets away, I must see him somewhere or other, I thought. Why hadn't I bumped into him again yet?

That evening when I was helping Anette and Robert, and my sister was endlessly groaning what a great effort moving is, it suddenly struck me that Tom had probably only recently moved to the area. For a moment I was optimistic again.

I had plenty of time on my hands over the next two weeks. Dietmar was ill in bed with a **sore throat**, and so extra tuition had been cancelled. A few times I asked Tanja whether she would like to come and see me in the afternoon, but she always had some appointment or other as an excuse. To **distract** myself, I went to football training on a Tuesday after-

---

sore throat – Halsentzündung; to distract – ablenken

noon after a long absence, and was totally shocked to read a note at the sports hall saying that our team had decided to **disband** at the end of the month.

"What are we supposed to do," sighed Uli, our trainer who was just opening up the hall. "It's only natural. Girls of your age have just got boys in their heads. During the last few weeks hardly any one of you came for training."

Feeling guilty, I remained silent.

He smiled. "It's not your fault. Your father told me what problems you're having at school, and of course I understand that maths comes first. But it is a pity; you were such a good team. You would definitely have got **promotion**, especially with you in the attack. Just imagine, I might nearly have found a sponsor for you." He regarded me **pensively**. "You and your team, you could have been something big. But what the heck? I've got to go. Bye, Henri."

He gave me a friendly wave and ran to a group of girls who were waiting in front of the changing rooms. As I went past I heard him say: "You'll be a great team, I bet, and if you're really good, then I'll get a super sponsor for you."

I grimaced. Right, it was the turn of the younger ones now. But one day there would be boys …

---

to disband – sich auflösen; promotion – Aufstieg; pensively – nachdenklich

Tanja was probably still a bit **miffed** that I'd hardly told her anything about Tom, I thought. So the next day, while we were waiting for the tram at lunchtime, I said without hesitation: "By the way, Tanja, it's all over with Tom."

There was no reaction from Tanja; instead she stared over the shoulder of an older man who was just reading a magazine.

"I said that it's over with Tom."

Tanja now turned to face me. "I thought so," she said coldly. "You asked me four times last week to come over and see you. Of course, I realized straight away that good old Tanja was just being used as a **stopgap**."

I swallowed. "No, it's not like that. I must tell you what really happened."

I intended telling Tanja the whole truth, but my friend just waved me aside. "Spare me with your stories about boys; I've got enough problems of my own." She was silent for the rest or the journey.

But in the afternoon she did ring me up. It was silly to argue over such a small thing, she said, and that we should **stick together**. I agreed with her immediately.

"Do you reckon you'll be able to come to Berlin?" she then asked.

I didn't understand what she was talking about, at first.

---

miffed – verstimmt, verärgert; stopgap – Lückenbüßer;
to stick together – zusammenhalten

"We had planned go to Berlin together in the summer holidays," she reminded me, and from the tone in her voice I could tell that she was starting to get annoyed again.

I said that my parents had almost already agreed, and I just couldn't wait to see Ronald Reimann.

Tanja laughed bitterly. "Ronald Reimann. Don't talk about him! You've got no idea what's going on."

While sobbing, she told me that Ronald Reimann had got married at New Year, and had moved with his wife to the Bahamas. "He's married a blonde, not a true blonde, of course, and my mother says she's had **plastic surgery** at least five times."

"Then why on earth should we be going to Berlin?" I asked. "I mean, when your Ronald Reimann is sitting in the Bahamas."

"You know the 'Heidhoferstraße', don't you? Well, after the shock, I didn't want to watch any more episodes, but then I forced myself, thank God. The new tenant in flat 7 is really sweet. I can tell you, compared with Harry Willings, that's his name, Reimann is absolutely nothing. The day before yesterday I wrote to Harry, asking him for his autograph. And guess what, Harry also happens to live in Berlin. Isn't that absolutely brilliant? We don't have to change our travel plans at all."

All the time I just nodded my head. Then we

---

plastic surgery – Schönheitsoperation

would just wait around in Berlin for Harry instead, I didn't mind.

"You're not saying anything," complained Tanja who, logically, was not aware that I'd been nodding my head.

"I think it's great," I insisted, and promised to watch "Heidhoferstraße" that very evening, and to look out only for Harry Willings.

How fortunate that there were still a few months to go until the summer holidays. Perhaps Harry Willings would get married at Easter and then move to the Bahamas. Tanja's next **heart-throb** could live somewhere around here for a change.

Actually, I was going to write Tom off, but then my sister Babette gave me an idea. She phoned to say that she wouldn't be able to come home next weekend, unfortunately, as she had a job babysitting.

"You as a babysitter?" I asked in surprise. "And what are you going to do with the kid? Count **building blocks**?"

Babette laughed. "It's totally harmless," she said. "The kid is three months old and is a real **screamer**. He's only quiet when he's being taken for a walk in the **pram**. So I'm going to take the baby out for a two hours' walk every afternoon, earn lots of lovely money doing it, and make a young mother happy

---

heart-throb – Schwarm; building blocks – Bausteine; screamer – Schreihals; pram – Kinderwagen

who would otherwise have a nervous breakdown sooner or later."

All good things come in threes. Plan number three was beginning to develop: I would look for a job where I could stay outside, despite the cold, damp weather. I would have to bump into Tom sooner or later. A job as a babysitter would be ideal. Just like my sister I would wander around the streets with a pram every afternoon.

The biggest problem now was to find parents who would trust me with their child. In the newspaper there were adverts for at least five **surrogate grandmothers**. There was no demand for a highly motivated school girl, it seemed. Alright then, I would just go for a little walk on my own. Three quarters of an hour in the afternoon, I tramped through the wet **slush** – of course without a trace of Tom. Instead Mum discovered me just as she was leaving work, and she bundled me straight into the car and drove me home.

"Your feet are soaking wet," she **scolded**. "Don't be surprised if you're ill again. Stuff your shoes with newspaper straight away, otherwise they won't dry."

Instead of being pleased that I was out in the fresh air and not sitting in front of the television, she just moans at me, I thought annoyed, and at the very same moment I let out a **shriek**. Here was exactly

---

surrogate grandmother – Ersatzoma; slush – Schneematsch; to scold – schimpfen; shriek – spitzer Schrei

what I'd been looking for. I carefully smoothed out the half-crumpled newspaper that I was about to stuff into my left boot. "Help! Prevented through illness. Who will take Archimedes out for a walk every afternoon from 3 until 4 o'clock? Please **apply** to Engel, Rilkestraße 18."

Rilkestraße 18, that was nearby. Whoever Archimedes might be, I would take him for a walk every day.

An hour later I had my job. I was to take the **long-haired dachshund** Archimedes for a walk seven days a week, until the proud owner, Mrs Engel, could walk without **crutches** again.

"But please ask your parents whether you are allowed to," said Mrs Engel when I took my leave of her and Archimedes.

Mum and Dad will certainly be glad if I get out in the fresh air every day, I thought to myself on the way home. But I was mistaken, once again.

"Taking a dog out," said Mum with a **disapproving** look, "the ideas you get, Henriette!"

"Babette is running all over Freiburg with a pram, and you don't say anything about that," I **objected**. "A dog is totally harmless in comparison!"

Mum looked at me inquiringly. "What do you mean harmless? A dog can bite, it can be bitten by bigger dogs, anything at all might happen. Do some

---

to apply – sich bewerben; long-haired dachshund – Langhaardackel; crutches – Krücken; disapproving – missbilligend; to object – einwenden more work in the household instead, and then we'll increase your pocket money."

"But it's not about money. I just want to get out in the fresh air a bit more," I **burst out**.

Mum stared at me. "You say something!" she requested Dad.

"Perhaps a bit of fresh air will do her good," said Dad. "I think Henri is looking rather **pale**. How big is the animal that you're going to be taking out?"

I flung my arms around Dad's neck, assured him that Archimedes was the smallest and sweetest long-haired dachshund you could imagine, and promptly rang up Mrs Engel to tell her that my parents had given their permission.

The next afternoon, shortly before I set off to collect Archimedes, Tanja rang up. She wanted to tell me the latest about Harry Willings.

"I'm sorry, Tanja, I haven't got time at the moment," I said. "I've got to go."

Tanja swallowed. "Are you meeting anyone?"

I laughed and promised to tell her everything the next day **in minute detail**.

She would probably be expecting a love story. I would tell her about my walk with Archimedes. "He looks fantastic," I could say, "long black hair, dark brown eyes, not very tall, and slightly **bow-legged**.

---

to burst out – herausplatzen; pale – blass; in minute detail – in allen Einzelheiten; bow-legged – o-beinig

But the best thing about him is his faithful **doggy look**." I had to laugh out loud.

"He likes variety," Mrs Engel had told me when I picked up Archimedes. "That means he doesn't always want to go to the same tree."

I promised to show Archimedes new trees all the time, not to go anywhere near butchers and taxi ranks (Archimedes didn't like taxi drivers, for some **inexplicable** reason) and to be back at the garden gate punctually at four o'clock. *With* Archimedes, as Mrs Engel **emphasised** several times.

"And remember, Henriette. He must never be allowed to get bored," Mrs Engel reminded me once again.

I nodded and set off with the dachshund on the **lead**. I wanted to **tick off** the first three streets on my plan. That way, I'll be giving him enough variety, I said to myself, although to be really honest, I was only doing it so that I might bump into Tom.

During my daily walks with Archimedes, I had plenty of time to think. It still wasn't clear to me why Tom had offered to bring me my purse. I had thought of three possibilities.

The first one was that Tom was a naturally polite and **obliging** sort of person, in which case, he couldn't have behaved any differently.

Another possibility was that he wanted to crawl to

---

doggy look – Hundeblick; inexplicable – unerklärlich;
to emphasise – betonen; lead – Leine; to tick off – abhaken;
obliging – hilfsbereit

Dietmar and Caberg, so that he would be given easier problems to solve during extra tuition, in return for small services such as running after **scatterbrained** girls with their belongings.

The third possibility was the most **enticing**: Tom remembered me and was looking for an opportunity to get into conversation with me.

But how was I supposed to find out why Tom had really come?

Archimedes tugged on his lead.

"Yes, yes, alright, you **sausage dog**," I muttered, and let him sniff around four lampposts and a wall, and bark at a large **tabby cat** that was sitting on a balcony and staring down suspiciously from a safe distance.

I'll take my walkman with me next time, I swore to myself, because to be honest, the walks with Archimedes were pretty boring. How Mrs Engel came to think that her dachshund needed variety, I don't know. He sometimes sniffed around the same corner for minutes on end until he finally lifted his leg.

Archimedes had chosen a new tree at last, and tugged me on. Pinned to the tree was a bright red poster saying "Come to our big **fancy-dress** carnival party".

Indeed, the football club was organizing its annual

---

scatterbrained – schusselig; enticing – verlockend;
sausage dog – Dackel; tabby cat – Tigerkatze; fancy-dress – Kostüm, Verkleidung

ball. Last year my team performed a sketch of cleaning ladies doing a ballet dance. There was even a photograph of us all in the newspaper, showing how we did the dance, equipped with buckets and brooms. It was a pity that the team no longer existed.

A car passed me at such a great speed that slush splashed everywhere. Annoyed, I turned around. And then I discovered *him.* Tom was standing at the roadside some distance away. He was carrying an longish parcel under his arm, and was looking around, undecided. Was he waiting for someone?

"Hello, Tom!" I wanted to call out, but I just didn't dare. We didn't know each other well enough yet for me to call out to him from this distance. I'll just **casually** walk up to him, and start up a conversation, I decided. My voice will sound quite calm, and he won't notice how much my heart is pounding.

You just have to convince yourself, Dad says sometimes, and then it all works out.

But first I had to **tear** Archimedes away from this tree. However, no matter how hard I tried to persuade him, he just wouldn't move from the spot. He behaved like a stubborn old **mule**, and became at least as strong. I pulled the lead, but the stupid sausage dog just growled at me **reluctantly**, and then raised his leg again. How could such a little creature **pee** so often?

---

casually – locker, lässig; to tear – ziehen; mule – Maultier, Esel; reluctantly – widerstrebend; to pee – pinkeln

I was just about to pull the little **mutt** away from the tree, regardless of the consequences, when Mrs Engel's **lodger**, of all people, turned up. He **pounced on** Archimedes enthusiastically. "How lovely for dear little Archimedes to get out again," said the old man. "Such a lovely animal. And he's not just an ordinary dog. My wife, who died last year, sadly, wanted to knit him a little coat for the cold winter days."

He became silent and gazed at Archimedes who was now having to go sniffing around the streets without a coat in spite of the cold.

I smiled amiably and was going to turn around but the man grasped my arm firmly. "Don't make any sudden movements, young lady, Archimedes might misunderstand. One day I was going to refill his bowl, and then snap" – he moved his arm swiftly through the air, causing the dachshund to jump with fright – "snap, he had already bitten me."

"I think I've got to go back," I apologized, "it's almost quarter to four, and Mrs Engel …"

"**How convenient**," said the man, "I'm on my way home, too. So much nicer in pleasant company such as yours."

I made an effort to smile, and looked down the street. Of course, there was not a sign of Tom, far and wide. If the old man hadn't stopped me, I would

---

mutt – Köter; lodger – Untermieter; to pounce on – sich stürzen auf; how convenient – das trifft sich gut

now be standing at the other end of the street, having a nice chat to Tom.

For three minutes he was telling me all about his deceased wife, and how nice Mrs Engel was. It then **occurred** to him that he'd wanted to go to the **barber's shop**, in fact, so he couldn't accompany me on the way home, and he hastily said goodbye.

I was furious. I had missed a **unique** opportunity. With a dog on a lead, it was easy to start a conversation with other people. Maybe Tom would have asked me if it was my dog, and might even have offered to accompany me on the dog walks. But this stupid mutt had **spoiled** everything!

I was still standing in front of the poster announcing the fancy-dress ball. I read the words for the tenth time at least. "This year's motto: a fairy tale ball!" The new girls' football team would do a ballet dance dressed up as cleaning ladies, much to the delight of the audience. "Huh," I said so loud that Archimedes growled in surprise, huh, **see if I care**!

I glanced at my watch. Just before four, high time to take the dog home. I glanced back to see if Tom had miraculously re-appeared, but the street was completely empty.

I sullenly stomped along next to Archimedes, who was in rather a hurry all of a sudden to get home to his mistress.

---

to occur – einfallen; barber's shop – Herrenfrisör;
unique – einzigartig; to spoil – verderben;
see if I care – mir doch egal

"What **were you up to** yesterday afternoon then? Go on, tell me," Tanja greeted me the next morning on the tram, and squeezed into the seat next to me. "Anything to do with a boy?"

Actually, I had wanted to tease Tanja with that silly joke about the doggy eyes, but I decided not to bother. Tanja might **take offence**. So I told the truth about what had happened yesterday afternoon and the strange old man. I didn't say a word about Tom, though.

Tanja shook her head. "How annoying. I was just about to go out, and then my mum came home, **thoroughly fed up** because she's having problems with her new boyfriend. And then she'd drunk a bit too much because her horoscope was particularly bad that day and … well, you know what it's like." Tanja looked at me meaningfully. "I don't know why you bother doing it at all. Is it because of the cash?"

I mumbled something or other. It was fortunate that Tanja wasn't interested in me any longer.

"There's something I really must tell you: I've invited Daniel to my birthday party so that there'll be about the same number of boys and girls. Simon might come as well and bring a friend with him. I was thinking of you a bit, I mean now that you and Tom …" She was kind enough to say no more.

Thanks, Tanja, how charming of you, I thought,

---

to be up to sth – etwas vorhaben; to take offence – übel nehmen; thoroughly fed up – vollkommen fertig

and felt how angry I was getting. Just so that I wouldn't sit around like a **wet blanket** all evening, she had invited Daniel and Simon and his friend, and God knows whoever else.

"I only wanted to do you a favour," Tanja said. "And anyway, Evelyn and her boyfriend, Christiane, Nadja, Gerd ..." She listed half the class. "If everything is alright again between you and Tom, then bring him along. There are **mounds and mounds of** sausage and noodle salad. And I've got at least fourteen pizzas on standby." She took a deep breath. "Don't you think you could bring Tom anyway? I mean, even if it is all over between you."

I must have had a **daft** look on my face, because Tanja hastened to add that it wasn't all that important, but if Tom could play the violin so well, then perhaps he might play something at her party. At Evelyn's birthday party, **apparently**, a whole band had performed.

I promised Tanja I would think about it, and was just about to suggest that Christiane could **do a party piece** with her flute, when she interrupted me.

"Oh damn, look," she pointed at Dr Caberg who was just getting out of her car with a **pile** of poisonous-green exercise books under her arm. "She'll be giving our maths tests back today."

We'd had the maths test at the beginning of the

---

wet blanket – Trauerkloß; mounds and mounds of – Unmengen von; daft – blöde; apparently – angeblich; to do a party piece – auftreten; pile – Stapel

week on Monday. I hadn't mentioned it at home. I wanted to wait for the result first. I hadn't got involved with the usual speculations after the test this time either. I just wanted to surprise myself. The grade can't be too bad, I had thought, because that would mean Dietmar's extra tuition was no good.

"I bet I've got an E," moaned Tanja **under her breath**, when Caberg put the exercise books on the desk in the first lesson. "I've worked it out. With seven out of a possible twenty marks, that means an E plus. And my mother only ever looks at the E, and never sees the plus sign."

Just this once Tanja had calculated correctly. I saw how she turned pale as she opened up her exercise book.

"And what about you? Let's have a look," she asked, and glanced over my shoulder. "B to C."

"*You see, you can do it!*" Caberg had scribbled next to it.

"It's alright for you," Tanja sighed, and stuffed her maths exercise book back into her rucksack.

Out of habit I added up the marks and **stopped short**. Yes, Caberg really had given me two marks too many. She had never made a mistake in our favour before. Did it have anything to do with my extra tuition with her son, perhaps? I decided not to say anything, preferring to copy the English

---

under one's breath – halblaut; just this once – ausnahmsweise; to stop short – stutzen, aufmerken

homework from Christiane that I had completely forgotten.

Tanja was rather **subdued** all morning.

"My mother is **blackmailing** me," she confided in me during the main break when we sneaked off to buy some bread rolls from the baker's next door. "Yeah, just imagine, she'll only let me go to Berlin if I don't get two E's in my half-yearly report," she wailed. "That's utterly childish. It's not my fault if I only understand just a bit in maths, and nothing at all in English. It's beginning to give me an upset stomach." She took a hearty bite of her bread roll, and looked at me expectantly. "What would you do?"

"Perhaps you should have extra tuition, too," I suggested without thinking. "In English, of course," I added in alarm, because if Tanja was going to Dietmar … it didn't **bear** thinking about. Tanja would never forgive me for all my fibs.

"Don't worry, I'm not gong to pinch Tom off you. But then again, it's all over between you two, isn't it?" she asked suspiciously.

"Tanja, forget it please, it's all far more complicated than you can imagine," I begged her. "Let's think instead how we can make the holiday in Berlin work, at least."

By the end of the break we realized that Tanja had only *one* chance: She had to **work on** either the English teacher or Dr Caberg.

---

subdued – niedergeschlagen; to blackmail – erpressen; to bear – ertragen; to work on sb – jmd. bearbeiten

"Well? What d'you reckon? Who should I talk to?" asked Tanja during the next short break.

I had thought about the matter thoroughly. Even though I wasn't all that mad about going to Berlin, especially with the prospect of having to wait around all day for the redheaded **midget** from "Heidhofer-straße", I was obliged to help Tanja. She's my best friend, the only one in fact, and even if she really can get on my nerves sometimes, I still like her. And anyway, it was a small **penance** for all that story-telling of mine lately.

I thought it would be best to work on Caberg, and suggested we should wait for her after the sixth lesson. "Gersner is a tough nut," I tried to persuade her, "you'll be lucky if he even gives you an E. It's a waste of time talking to that teacher."

Tanja nodded. Achim Gersner, our English teacher is by far the most **unpopular** teacher at all the schools within a radius of fifty kilometres. "He's a career freak," my sisters had already grumbled years ago. It was a fact that he wasn't the sort of person to **turn** even **the blindest eye** to anything, and so Tanja's only chance lay in the hands of Dr Caberg.

"What should I say to her then?" moaned my friend when we were waiting in the car park in front of the school after the sixth lesson. I mean, I can't just go

---

midget – Knirps; penance – Buße; unpopular – unbeliebt; to turn a blind eye – ein Auge zudrücken

and say please don't give me an E. After all, I'm halfway between a D and an E at the moment."

"The best thing is you keep out of it completely," I said, "just leave it to me. And anyway, you're not halfway between a D and an E, but three quarters to E."

Tanja rolled her eyes. "Alright, if that's what you reckon. And if you can persuade Caberg, then get on with it as far as I'm concerned. D'you think she's coming today?" She frowned at her watch. "After all, we've been waiting here for twelve, no, eighteen minutes."

I saw the two of them first. Caberg was hurrying along the long **glazed** corridor, and Dietmar was carrying a pile of books behind her. If he were to greet me and say anything about my maths test, then Tanja would notice that something was not right. I tugged at her sleeve.

"Tanja, I don't think it was such a very good idea, after all. We'll be making a huge mistake if we wait for Caberg here," I **implored** her. "She's tired, hungry, it's the wrong time of the month, and who knows what else. And when she sees the two of us here, she'll immediately know that we are trying **to get around her**. Besides, perhaps one of the other teachers, or even the headmaster will see her here with us, and draw his own conclusions. Nobody must

---

glazed – verglast; to implore – beschwören;
to get around sb – jmd. rumkriegen

notice what we're up to. I've got a much better plan. Come on, let's go."

Reluctantly, Tanja allowed herself to be led away from the car park. She grumbled why hadn't it occurred to me half an hour earlier, but she saw that I was right. I promised to take care of the matter in the afternoon, and to ring her up as soon as I had been able to **achieve** something.

---

to achieve – erreichen

A delivery van

was standing in our parking space when I arrived home, almost an hour late. Babette was sitting in it together with a **bloke** with a **moustache**. It took them both half an eternity to notice me standing directly in front of the car. And it took just as long for me to realize that the pair of them were staring into Babette's new laptop.

"Henri, how wonderful that you've come at last," shouted Babette, who had opened the car door energetically. "We've been waiting over an hour. Anthony and I are absolutely frozen stiff. I can't find my key to the door," she explained, when she noticed that I didn't understand what was going on.

"And who's Anthony, may I ask?" I said quietly as I opened the door.

"I met Anthony at a congress. In London," she whispered. "But there's no harm in talking louder. He doesn't understand a word of German."

She waved to Anthony who was carefully locking

---

bloke – Typ, Kerl; moustache – Schnurrbart

up the van, checking the doors for the second time. "He's a bit eccentric at times, but a brilliant mathematician," she enthused. "I thought I'd bring him with me. The half-yearly report is just around the corner. It'll do you some good to speak a bit of English."

I smiled at my sister gratefully. It was really good to know how unselfish she was. She really had gone and found a true Englishman, all just to help her little sister.

"And what do you want in return for this generous help?" I inquired suspiciously.

Babette waved Anthony into the house, and **steered** him past me into the living room, without saying a word. Perhaps *she* should start having conversation lessons with Anthony, I thought when I remembered that English had always been a bit of a problem subject with Babette, too.

"OK, what do you want for it?" I repeated my question, and followed Babette into the kitchen where she hurriedly put the kettle on for tea.

"Anthony is on holiday and I'm on **vacation**. Of course, we've both got loads of work to do …"

"What do you want?" I interrupted her, giving her an icy look.

"Well, we'd like to stay here for a while, and my old room is a bit too small for the two of us. I thought you could let us have your room, and you could

---

to steer – steuern; vacation – hier: Semesterferien

move into my old room for the time being." She looked at me imploringly. "Anthony's brought you a brilliant CD."

The pair of them could stay in my room, as far as I was concerned. I just couldn't wait to see Mum and Dad's faces when they discovered our new resident that evening.

"Yeah, OK," I said. "but please **spare me with** English lessons with Anthony. And don't go giving Mum and Dad any ideas."

Babette flung her arms around my neck, and said that she'd always known that she had a fantastic sister.

"What's going on here?" called Dad on the staircase when he came home with Mum.

"What's supposed to be going on?" I called back.

"Well, what's that van doing in our parking space," inquired Mum. "Are we moving out **by** any **chance**?"

Babette came rushing out of the living room, and flung her arms around her neck. "No, of course not. Anthony and I have got it from a friend who's away on holiday for a few weeks. It's all completely harmless, really."

Now that my parents had got over the initial shock, I thought, they probably wouldn't be too bothered about Anthony. And that's how it was.

---

to spare sb with sth – jmd. mit etwas verschonen;
by chance – zufällig

They seemed really pleased about the prospect of having Anthony and Babette visiting them for weeks. I found out why, while I was **clearing** some of my things into Babette's old room.

"It sounds very promising indeed," I heard Mum whisper. "He's got a doctorate and a permanent post at the university. Makes a change from all the **drop-outs** that Babette has brought home so far. Can you remember the one who used to play the guitar all day?" She laughed quietly. "I *am* pleased that Babette is becoming sensible at last."

The guitar player! I can still remember Markus very well. Babette turned up with him two years ago, and I'd fallen in love with him immediately. In the afternoons I used to sit down next to him for hours, listening to him play Irish ballads. At some point or other my sister got fed up with sharing her boyfriend with her little sister. She promised me five euros if I left the room at last. But I was **steadfast**. I wouldn't have let Markus out of my sight, not for all the money in the world. Unfortunately, the relationship finished after a few weeks – Babette insisted that it was my fault – and Markus never appeared on the scene again.

So now there was Anthony. He wasn't my taste, but then again it was Babette who had to be happy with him. I smiled at myself in the mirror that I found in

---

to clear – räumen; drop-out – Studienabbrecher; steadfast – standhaft

her desk. Wasn't I extremely selfless? **Fate** would now have to take pity on me at last, and let Tom turn up. My eyes fell on the pocket watch that was lying in the desk drawer.

Heaven's above, quarter past three! I'd completely forgotten all about Archimedes. I pulled on my anorak as **quick as lightning**, and marched off.

Mrs Engel opened the door indignantly. "It's not quite half-past two, Henriette dear. Archimedes and I are having our **afternoon nap**. Come on time at three o'clock."

The watch in Babette's desk was still set to summer time, and I, silly idiot, had **fallen for it**. But it was not worth going home any more. I strolled along the street and observed a woman wrapped-up warmly, sticking up posters.

I knew the poster. "Come to our big fancy-dress carnival party – this year's motto: a fairy tale ball," I read.

The woman noticed that she was being **observed**, and turned around.

"Isn't that you, Henri?" she asked. "Of course it is. I recognize you now. You probably don't remember me. I'm your former coach's wife."

I mumbled something like "Oh yeah," and she laughed at me happily. "What an awful job this is

---

fate – das Schicksal; quick as lightning – blitzschnell; afternoon nap – Mittagsschlaf; to fall for sth – auf etwas reinfallen; to observe – beobachten

There's some kind of invitation stuck to every tree. But our posters are obviously the best ones." She nodded with satisfaction. "Uli designed it. He's a good coach, but he's just fantastic at graphic art. Don't you think so?"

I was able to nod with a clear conscience. Uli really was a good coach.

His wife took a deep breath. "But it's still an awful lot of work putting up all the posters and **distributing** personal invitations. You can take yours with you now. That saves me one journey."

She pulled an envelope out of her shoulder bag. "Here you are, the Schneider family, five tickets. Without tickets it costs twelve euros per person at the **evening box office**."

At first I wanted to say that I didn't feel like going to the fancy-dress ball at all, but I decided it would be better to remain silent. I didn't want to disappoint the woman.

"Have you got a bit of time, by any chance?" she asked. "I've still got eighteen invitations to deliver in this area, and I could do with some help."

"No, I've got to go," I explained. It was three minutes to three, and high time to pick up Archimedes.

"See you at the ball," she called after me, and looked for a suitable tree for her next poster.

---

to distribute – verteilen; evening box office – Abendkasse

The evening meal passed in silence because none of us felt like speaking English all the time.

All of a sudden I remembered the entrance tickets.

"By the way, it's the football club's fancy-dress ball on Saturday," I said, and pulled five slightly **crumpled** tickets out of my trouser pocket. "Are you going?"

Mum and Dad looked at each other **hesitantly**. "Actually, we wanted to go to the tennis-club ball," they said **in unison** and laughed. "But Babette, Anthony and you, you could all go."

Babette translated and explained in many details what "carnival time" is like in Germany, and Anthony pretended to be terribly enthusiastic. But I suspected that, as a true mathematician, he would much rather stay at home **doing sums**. You see, in the afternoon, when I had come back from my walk with Archimedes, I had caught him scribbling figures and letters on the wooden kitchen table because he hadn't found a clean sheet of paper.

"We'll have to **dress up**, of course," explained Babette.

Dad suggested that Anthony should go as a **nought**. But Babette was offended, and said that she certainly wasn't going to translate that, and that she was shocked at her father's strange sense of

---

crumpled – zerknittert; hesitantly – unschlüssig;
in unison – einstimmig; to do sums – rechnen;
to dress up – sich verkleiden; nought – Null

humour. Besides, she thought carnival was stupid anyway, and Anthony probably felt the same. "You can **stick** your stupid tickets," she shouted, dragging Anthony, who didn't understand a thing, out of the room.

Dad looked around uncomfortably.

"That wasn't quite right of you," Mum **rebuked** him gently, "you know how Babette is always so **quick to hit the roof**, and …"

"But I'm not going on my own," I interrupted her, "I'd feel stupid."

They both looked at me concerned. For a moment I thought I could read their minds: the poor child has lost all her self-confidence. She used to be quite different, so much more **adventurous**. What on earth is the matter?

Of course, not wanting to be regarded as a problem child, I quickly said: "I'll ask Tanja if she feels like coming with me."

"What a brilliant idea. Tanja is just the right company," said Mum, and Dad handed me the telephone straight away.

I looked at him, completely **flabbergasted**. They usually moaned at me for being too long on the phone, and now my father was placing the phone in front of me on the table, asking me to ring up Tanja straight away. It would be a shame if Tanja happened

---

to stick – sich an den Hut stecken; to rebuke – tadeln;
to be quick to hit the roof – schnell an die Decke gehen;
adventurous – abenteuerlustig; flabbergasted – entgeistert

to accept an invitation that very evening to visit her great aunt.

I dialled the number and went to my room. If my parents wanted to know what I was talking about with Tanja, they'd have to listen at the door.

I had hardly spoken my name when Tanja interrupted me.

"Don't say you've got tickets for the fairy tale ball," she shouted enthusiastically. "Will you take me with you?"

"Yes, of course, that's why I'm ringing," I said.

"Henri, you're a real friend," Tanja praised me, "I desperately need a bit of good news at the moment, you see. You can't imagine the crisis I'm just going through." She sniffed heavily. "You know my fantastic birthday party. I've got everything organized already, everyone's been invited, and now my dear brother says that it's all a bit **over the top**, and I should celebrate in the afternoon with two friends – girls. He's completely mad. He suggests playing silly party games and all that kind of kids' rubbish." She sniffed again. "Hang on a moment, I desperately need a clean paper handkerchief."

She gave her nose a good blow three times before she continued moaning. "My mother was easily influenced, of course, and said I should have my party in the summer when we can go outside. Just be glad

---

over the top – eine Nummer zu groß

that you don't have a brother, it's a real punishment."

"So does that mean you won't be celebrating your birthday until the summer?" I asked carefully.

"Exactly," said Tanja in a dark voice. "But who knows what will happen then. I've just got a streak of bad luck at the moment. Speaking of which, have you done anything about Caberg?"

Blast, I'd forgotten all about it. I **hesitated**. "I was just going to ring up, but I thought I'd ask you about the ball first."

I acted as though it had been very difficult to persuade my sister and her boyfriend to give up their tickets for Tanja.

"Henri, that's fantastic of you," Tanja kept saying, "my mother would never have allowed me to pay 12 euros for a ticket. Have you already thought about what you're going to wear?"

I confessed to Tanja that I hadn't really thought about it yet. She thought for a moment, and promised to ring me up if she had any ideas for a costume for me.

"And I'll sort everything out with Caberg," I promised.

Tanja didn't seem **to hold it against me**. "My horoscope mentions thunderclouds today, and it's true, at least as far as my party is concerned," she said. "Perhaps you should wait until tomorrow to ring up.

---

to hesitate – zögern; to hold sth against sb – jmd. etwas übel nehmen

You see, it says: a pleasing day ahead, in professional and private matters."

For a while we discussed how likely Caberg's decision was to be influenced by the horoscope. Tanja had to put the phone down to watch the next episode of "Heidhoferstraße". I don't think she was even angry with me for not saying anything about her latest redheaded heart-throb from the Heidhoferstraße.

I found Caberg's number in the telephone book, and dialled.

"Good evening, Mrs Caberg, I apologize for disturbing you so late," I started to say when the receiver was lifted after the third ring.

It was only quarter to seven, but I thought it sounded good as an introduction.

"Who's there?" snarled the voice at the other end of the line. I realized straight away that it was not Dr Caberg.

Slightly flabbergasted, I mumbled: "It's Henriette here." It would have been a disaster if I hadn't recognized Dietmar in time.

"I knew immediately," said Dietmar.

Stupid, I thought. Then why does he ask who's on the phone.

"It's kind of you to ring, though. I'm feeling better again, but I'm not allowed to talk too much. But I think we can continue with the lessons in about two or three weeks."

That's right, Dietmar had been ill. I had completely forgotten. I lied a bit about how pleased I was to be having extra tuition again soon, and asked if I could talk to his mother.

Dietmar asked if he might be able to help me. I explained to him that it was a very private matter, and I noticed how he was unsure for a moment.

"Yes, just a minute, I'll go and get her, she's in the cellar, I think," he stammered.

Then I heard nothing for a while.

I stared at the telephone book in front of me, and could hardly believe my eyes. During the last few minutes I had written Tom's name on the margin seven times. That would be a field day for my nosey sister Babette, I thought, and drew big black hearts over the name. I had to be careful not to talk about Tom in my sleep.

Where on earth was Caberg? I must have been waiting for ten minutes.

Through the phone I could hear voices, indistinctly. About time too.

"Caberg," answered my maths teacher. "Any problems, Henriette?"

"Yes, I'm a bit worried about my grade in the half-yearly report," I claimed. "I've added up all the marks from tests, and I'm on the border line."

Caberg laughed. "Henriette, I can give you a B with an easy conscience. Your oral work has been good recently, and I did mark the last test a bit **on the tough side**."

---

on the tough side – hart, streng

Brilliant. Fantastic.

It was working out much better than I had dared to dream.

"That's why I'm ringing up," I said, trying to sound **crestfallen**. "Unfortunately, you miscounted by two marks. In my favour!"

Caberg was silent for a moment. I could imagine how she was frowning.

"Well," she said finally, "that won't make much difference to your grade. Anything else?"

I noticed how she was gradually becoming impatient. Hastily I said: "Yes, and my friend Tanja has got a similar problem. She's just on the border line, and she's worried about getting an E."

I held my breath in suspense. Caberg didn't have any choice, she just had to give Tanja a D.

"You can reassure Tanja she doesn't have to worry about anything," she said promptly.

I had the impression that she was rather annoyed, but there was nothing else she could do. If I told everyone in the class that I had two marks too many, and that was the only reason I managed to a get a B, there would be an awful lot of trouble. If it then became known I was having extra lessons with her son, Caberg could start packing her bags. But our maths teacher is an intelligent woman. She knew exactly what was what.

"Thank you, Dr Caberg. I told Tanja that it is pos-

---

crestfallen – niedergeschlagen

sible to talk to you," I crawled, and wished her and Dietmar a pleasant evening.

Satisfied, I strolled back into the living room and studied the television guide. After a minute the phone rang. Dad pointed his finger at me, without saying a word.

"I would have rung you in a few minutes," I said to Tanja who sounded very **distraught**. "But I first had to recover from the phone call with Caberg."

"I knew it would all go wrong," Tanja lamented. "My mother will **go bananas** when she sees the two E's."

I laughed. "She won't have to. Unless Caberg is a bit **malicious** – and I don't think she is – she's going to give you a D. I've just had quite a sensible conversation with her."

Tanja **whooped** with delight. "Do you really think I'm going to get around the E? Henriette, I'll never forget you for this. If you want, I'll give you Ronald Reimann's autograph with the gold frame. And I'll be much, much nicer to Caberg in future.

I generously **declined** the autograph, asked Tanja not to tell a soul about my conversation with Caberg, and put the phone down, exhausted. It was now time to think about myself again.

Babette and her Anthony didn't **put in an appearance** for the whole evening. It was better that way,

---

distraught – verzweifelt; to go bananas – ausflippen; malicious – heimtückisch; to whoop – jubeln; to decline – ablehnen; to put in an appearance – sich blicken lassen

too, as nobody could steal the show from me when I casually mentioned: "By the way, we got our maths test back today."

Mum hurriedly closed her laptop. Dad put his financial newspaper aside and sat up straight, as if to say the pleasant part of the evening is over.

"Well?" both of them asked, almost in unison.

"Well," I said. "I'd best go and get it for you so you can have a look for yourselves."

I ran into my room out of habit. I'd already opened the door before I remembered that Babette and her boyfriend were now living there. I apologized quickly. But actually, it wasn't necessary. They were both sitting at the desk gazing into Babette's laptop. A fine love that is, I thought and sighed. I rummaged around in my wardrobe a bit, muttered "sorry" again, and returned to the living room. My parents were already **pacing up and down** between the balcony door and the radiator.

"Henriette, we won't scold you, really we won't," Mum reassured me, and her voice sounded a little bit uncertain.

I was surprised to discover that my parents really were worried.

"Everything's alright," I reassured them, "I've got a B to C."

Dad dropped back onto the sofa. "There you are then," he said satisfied, "you'd have been the first

---

to pace up and down – hin und her tigern

member of the family not to **cope** with figures. I think extra tuition is money well spent, after all." He went back to his newspaper, satisfied.

Mum said she'd like to see the B to C with her very own eyes. She had to sign it, anyway, or isn't that usual any more. I fetched my exercise book from my school bag in Babette's room. My mother breathed out quietly when she saw the grade and Caberg's **scribble**.

"I'm sorry, Henri," she then said, "but for a moment I had a horrible suspicion that you were **fooling us**." She hesitated briefly. "You know, you've been acting a bit different lately, and you read so much in the papers ..." She looked over to Dad, **beseechingly**, who put his newspaper down on the coffee table, with a regretful expression.

"Well, whatever," he came to her assistance, "Henri is growing up, after all. I think she has deserved a reward for her maths test. Is there anything you want in particular?

I thought for a moment. Of course, there were things that I wished for, it was only natural. Perhaps it was the right moment to talk about Berlin.

"Tanja and I would like to go to Berlin for a few days in the summer holidays," I said carefully. "Tanja's brother is coming, too."

"We weren't thinking about that kind of wish,

---

to cope – zurechtkommen; scribble – Gekritzel;
to fool sb – jmd. täuschen; beseechingly – flehentlich

actually," objected Dad. "Berlin is a big city and Tanja and you, well, you're not even fourteen yet. That's much too dangerous. And anyway, Tanja's brother has certainly got something better to do than look after you two. Ask for a new pair of trainers, or a computer game or something like that."

"I'll think about it," I said yawning. "I'll certainly have an idea tomorrow. I'm just too tired today."

I saw how Dad looked at Mum **reproachfully**. "You see, the child is suffering under all that **competitive pressure**," I heard him say. I didn't understand Mum's reply.

---

reproachfully – vorwurfsvoll;
competitive pressure – Leistungsdruck

i probably

caught a cold yesterday afternoon, I thought when I woke up the next morning with a slight sore throat.

It was fortunate that it had been the last walk with Archimedes. Mrs Engel was now better so that she could look after her dog on her own. And these walks hadn't **achieved** anything. Not once did I meet Tom. There was only one thing left for me to do: I had to forget him.

Anthony had cooked a real English breakfast for the whole family. "I hope you like it," he said in English. That was the first sentence I heard him speak.

Babette almost burst with pride when Dad exclaimed that that was exactly what he'd wanted: breakfast just like in England. Lately, he'd always been moaning about his **cholesterol**, but this morning he **polished off** the fried eggs and sausages without **batting an eyelid**.

---

to achieve – etwas einbringen; cholesterol – Blutfettwerte; to polish off – verputzen; to bat an eyelid – mit der Wimper zucken

"Henri, don't you like it?" she asked concerned when I was still nibbling at my first piece of toast after ten minutes.

"I think I'm ill," I said. "Mum, can you ring up school? I'm going back to bed."

"You don't look all that ill to me," determined Babette. "You just want to **skive off school**."

Stupid Babette! She was a snake, and I did let her have my lovely room after all. I poked my tongue out at her, behind Mum's back.

"Please leave Henriette alone," Mum scolded. "She is terribly **delicate** this winter, perhaps she just needs a good rest to completely recover."

"Babette and Anthony will have to look after you," Dad called after me, as I **swayed** into my room. "We've got a Japanese delegation coming to see us this afternoon at work. We might be late."

I didn't care. And the fact that Babette and Anthony would look after me didn't bother me, either. I got into bed and slept until lunchtime.

I felt much better then. I was just thinking that Babette and her boyfriend could perhaps do a bit of looking after me by making a nice lunch, when the phone rang. "I think she's still asleep. But I'll go and have a look." A second later the door to my room flew open. "Someone on the phone for you."

"Can you make me something to eat?" I asked her

---

to skive off school – Schule schwänzen; delicate – anfällig; to sway – schwanken

reproachfully. "After all, the pair of you are supposed to be looking after me."

Babette pulled a face, and handed me the phone. "Just be grateful that I take your phone calls," she whispered.

"Are you ill?" Tanja wanted to know.

I mumbled: "No, of course not. I just had something better to do this morning than go to school."

She laughed. "You really missed something today. Someone from the 12th **form** rammed Caberg's car. You should have seen her face when Zeynep suddenly appeared in the middle of the lesson and said: "Dr Caberg, Benjamin Hölter from form 12b has just driven into your car. I saw it."

"What?" I said in disbelief. "You're joking."

Tanja swore that she was telling the whole truth, and I regretted not being in school that morning.

"Besides, I've got something to confess." Tanja hesitated a moment. "You know you told me that Tom is so good at playing the violin? Well, during break I wanted to say something nice to Caberg, and so I asked her if her son was taking part in that competition for young musicians, and whether he might be giving a concert."

Oh, Tanja, you promised to keep your mouth shut, I thought, but I didn't say anything. Tanja was **remorseful** enough as it was.

"Caberg gave me quite a strange look. She then

---

form – Klasse; remorseful – reumütig, zerknirscht

said that I'd got things mixed up. But I think she was just **embarrassed**. Especially because half the class was listening."

I assured my friend that certainly nobody knew what was going on, and she promised not to tell a soul about Tom Caberg's musical talent in the future.

"But the reason I'm ringing," she said relieved, "is that I wanted to talk to you about the fancy-dress ball. All I could think of for you was a cleaning lady. With an apron and bucket. That's what you did last year, isn't it? Or have you got a better idea?"

Of course, I didn't. Quite the opposite. I hadn't given it a thought, but I didn't have to rub that under Tanja's nose. "Yeah," I said, "I wanted to do something different. I'm going to go as a **sailor**."

"As a sailor?" she asked.

"Yep, exactly. I'll put on some old jeans, a blue and white striped T-shirt and a pair of flip-flops. And I might take my little cousin's swimming ring."

I was rather proud of this idea. I had recently read that most sailors aren't able to swim. And that way, I would stand out a bit from all the other sailors at the ball.

"And what about you? What are you going as?" I asked.

Tanja gave a slight cough. "I ordered a **crop top**

---

to be embarrassed – peinlich berührt sein; sailor – Matrose; crop top – bauchfreies Oberteil

from the catalogue last night, in gold by the way. And a pair of reddish-gold harem trousers to go with it. Henri, I bet it'll suit me perfectly. My mother was really enthusiastic when I showed it to her. A harem lady, that would really suit me, she said. And guess what, she's paying for both of them. The shoes are a bit of a problem, though. Of course, golden **strappy sandals** would be the best, but I haven't got any like that. I don't suppose you, or anyone else in your family, have got any by any chance?"

I assured her that nobody in our family possessed golden strappy sandals, and Tanja kept thinking, over and over again, until she came to the conclusion that her father could, in fact, make a contribution. "I'll ring him up straight away," she said, and hung up.

I stood up and went into the kitchen. I couldn't expect any lunch from Babette and her boyfriend. They were sitting in front of the computer and were creating endless rows of figures.

"Aren't you hungry?" I asked carefully in German, and then in English, but the pair of them simply ignored me.

I went to get the leftovers from breakfast out of the kitchen, and **had a think**. Tanja as a harem lady, and me as a sailor. It was still better than a cleaning lady, but hardly ideal. There are dozens of sailors at

---

strappy sandals – Riemchensandalen; to have a think – gründlich nachdenken

a fancy-dress party. Harem ladies, too, but obviously the boys would be far more interested in a harem lady revealing her belly than a sailor wearing a swimming ring with ducks on. It **bugged** me a lot. I had to have a different fancy-dress costume, and I already had an idea how to get it.

"Is our little one feeling better?" asked Mum and Dad in chorus when they came home tired in the evening.

I nodded to reassure them. "I'm feeling great," I said, "apart from the fact that I'm absolutely starving. Babette and Anthony didn't cook anything."

My sister, who had been trying to **sew** a button on Anthony's jacket for the last few minutes, said in protest: "A proper English breakfast like we had this morning should be enough for the whole day. And anyway, it's a well known fact you shouldn't eat too much if you're ill. It's unhealthy."

"I fed myself on bread and butter. There wasn't much else in the fridge," I said, looking pitiful.

Mum gave me a comforting glance. "Henriette, I'll make you a nice supper now."

"Wait, hang on a minute!" I exclaimed. A nice supper didn't suit me at all. I had a completely different request. It wouldn't harm Mum and Dad to have a bit of a guilty conscience, it would makes things easier.

---

to bug – wurmen; to sew – nähen

"Last night you said that I could ask for something I'd like," I said hurriedly.

Babette looked up with interest from her work. How stupid! She usually sat in front of the computer all day, and didn't take notice of anything, but now of all times, she was listening to everything. But I had to risk it, otherwise the opportunity was wasted.

"I'd like something for the fancy-dress party," I said. "A harem costume!"

For a moment it was all quiet, then they all burst out laughing at the same time. What fantastic parents, what a great sister. Anthony came to see what all the noise was about and stood at the door frame. Even though he didn't understand a word, I bet, he laughed along with them. I wanted to **slap** them all **across the face**.

"I'm sorry," said Dad, who was the first to notice that I was close to tears, "I'm sorry, but that just isn't you. A harem lady!"

He rolled his eyes dramatically, and Anthony laughed again. He probably thought that everyday life in a German family was tremendously funny. I felt how the tears were **pricking** my eyes.

"Come on, Henri," said my sister and shook her head gently, "last year you dressed up in your football kit, tied an apron around and took a scrubbing brush with you. You didn't **kick up a fuss** then. So

---

to slap sb across the face – jmd. ohrfeigen;
to prick – hier: brennen; to kick up a fuss – Theater machen

why all the bother now? How about going as a sailor?"

"Exactly, a sailor is a brilliant idea," Mum agreed with her, and sneaked a look at the clock. "Let's have something to eat first. It has been a hard day for all of us."

It sounded as though the final word had been said. I turned on my heel, and marched into my new room. Babette, the **bitch**, had just **stabbed me in the back**.

Not to mention my parents. Last night they were full of big promises, saying I could ask for something I'd like, and then this.

I envied Tanja for her mother who was willing to pay for a cool fancy-dress costume. On the other hand, Tanja had had a whole lot of stress while her parents were **getting divorced**. I decided to give my parents another teeny-weeny chance. But one thing was clear. I would never turn up as a silly sailor wearing a swimming ring next to Tanja all dolled up in her harem costume. I would rather **raid** my bank account, or sell all my school books.

If only I could persuade Dietmar to cancel the next few lessons, and just share the money with me? No, it was hopeless; boring Dietmar would never do anything like that. Anyway, I needed the money for my fancy-dress costume next week.

---

bitch – Miststück; to stab sb in the back – jmd. in den Rücken fallen; to get divorced – sich scheiden lassen; to raid – plündern, ausrauben

Should I ring up my grandparents and tell them how they were treating me at home, in the hope that they would send me something? No. They would probably tell me a long and detailed story about how they used to dress up for carnival sixty years ago. That wouldn't get me anywhere at all. I had to talk to Tanja. Perhaps she had a good idea.

I was just about to go and get the phone when I heard a knock. Mum poked her head around the door.

"May I?" she asked, and was already standing in the middle of the room. "I just wanted to have a little chat about the thing we were talking about before," she said, and examined the chaos on my desk. "By the way, you could search to death for anything in this **pigsty**."

I nodded, but didn't say a word.

"Henriette, we've got a few problems at the moment. First of all there's work, but we don't want to bother you with that. Secondly we've got Anette who wants to split up with Robert yet again and move in here. And thirdly, there's the **weird** relationship between Babette and Anthony."

For a moment it looked as though Mum was going to start crying, but she just twisted her mouth. "At any rate, we are pleased that you've **caught up** again at school. Now we don't want to have a silly argument about a fancy-dress costume now, do we?"

---

pigsty – Saustall; weird – merkwürdig, schräg;
to catch up – sich fangen

"No, we don't," I agreed with her, "but I don't want to go as a silly cleaning lady. Besides, you did say yesterday that I could ask for something. So please, I'd like to have a fantastic fancy-dress costume."

"Nobody in our family has ever been at all interested in fancy-dress costumes," she said. "That's why I don't understand why, all of a sudden, you …" My mother seemed to be quite **at a loss**. "You can still have a lot of fun with everyday clothes. You've just got to have the will to do it."

She wanted to put her arm around my shoulder, but I turned away.

"Alright," she said. "have a good look through your wardrobe. With a little bit of fantasy, you can make something out of anything."

"I'm supposed to have a good look through my wardrobe. Take a look at that!" I opened the wardrobe and looked at Tanja, embittered. She was just as shocked as I was.

"I wouldn't have believed it of your parents," said Tanja. "They've got enough money, after all."

I didn't feel like explaining to Tanja that it probably wasn't a question of money with my parents, but it was just the principle of the matter. Anyway, it wouldn't have made any difference at all to the fact that I didn't have anything suitable to wear for the fancy-dress ball.

---

to be at a loss – ratlos sein

"You can't go to the ball wearing any of that stuff there in the wardrobe," said Tanja after she had closely examined everything, shaking her head at the checked pleated skirt.

"What on earth am I going to do?" I sat on the floor, completely at a loss.

"Haven't you got a smart dress at least? An evening dress or something? How about your sisters?" asked Tanja. "You could go as queen of the night."

"Hey, that's the very idea!" I said after a while. "Babette certainly won't have an evening dress, and Anette's things are all at Robert's now. But my mother has got an evening dress. Long and black, with a **plunging neckline**."

"Well, go on then, go and get it," said Tanja in a good mood. "I knew that I would think of something brilliant."

For a tiny moment I felt a bit guilty when I took Mum's evening dress out of her wardrobe.

"That looks exquisite," Tanja was amazed when I showed her the dress. "Put it on!"

I slipped into the expensive dress.

Tanja shook her head. "Oh dear, oh dear." Tightening her lips, she pointed to the **hem** that was at least three centimetres too short.

"My mother is just a bit smaller than me," I said.

"D'you think it's all that noticeable with a long dress? It is only for carnival."

---

plunging neckline – tiefer Ausschnitt; hem – Saum

Tanja looked at me horrified. "With a long dress it is especially important," she said. "There's no way you can go looking like that. **Half-mast** is definitely out. But there is one possibility. You can take out the hem. If you iron the dress afterwards, nobody will notice that the hem has been let down."

"Without a sewing machine?" I asked doubtfully.

"No problem," said my friend. "I'll get you some earrings and I'll put some make-up on you. You'll look absolutely **gorgeous** then. Apart from …" She plucked at the top of the dress and looked at me meaningfully. "Well, the neckline is intended for a *bigger* bust."

"Babette has got a wonder bra," I giggled. "D'you think Anthony has already noticed the **deception**? Should I just borrow it?"

Tanja also giggled. "Even a wonder bra can't make something out of nothing!" Before I got annoyed, she added: "Don't worry about it. You'll get a bust, too, one of these days."

Because I couldn't find the key to Babette's room, I pushed the desk in front of the door. I didn't want Mum to catch me undoing the hem of her expensive black evening dress.

It was quite easy to undo the hem, but I had great difficulties in sewing it back up again. The material

---

half-mast – "Hochwasser"; gorgeous – toll, umwerfend; deception – Betrug

kept slipping away, and everything I sewed looked a bit **askew**, I felt.

"Henriette," Mum called in front of my door, "what are you up to? Why have you locked yourself in? Come on. We want to go for a walk. It's lovely weather. The sun is shining so nicely. And then we're going to Anette and Robert's for coffee."

"I've got things to do," I shouted back.

"Maths?" asked Dad.

I mumbled something indistinctly.

"Go on, come with us," Babette begged me. "Anthony is so much looking forward to a walk with the family."

"Can't you let me work in peace?" I said slowly and loudly. I didn't feel like going with them just to satisfy Anthony's image of a typical German family taking a walk in the afternoon. Babette moaned for a bit, and then I heard how the front door shut. Now I could iron the hem in peace.

I had just filled the **steam iron** with distilled water, as instructed, put up the ironing board, and was wondering whether it would be better to iron the material on the right side or inside out, when I heard the house door open. "Mum!" was my first thought. My mother had a sixth sense and had guessed what her daughter was up to, and would now catch me **red-handed**. How was I supposed to explain it all?

---

askew – schief und krumm; steam iron – Dampfbügeleisen; red-handed – auf frischer Tat

With trembling hands, I tried to stuff the evening dress up my sweatshirt, but it was too late!

The door to the living room opened and … there was Anthony standing in front of me.

He waved to me with a red skiing glove, and grinned apologetically. He then mumbled something like "love" and looked around searchingly. It took me some time to realize that Anthony was looking for his second glove. If he wondered why his girlfriend's youngest sister had a black dress stuffed up her light-blue washed out sweatshirt, he gave no sign of it. We looked for the glove together until Babette started ringing the door bell like mad, complaining. I was to open the door, she demanded, we were just too stupid to look.

I swallowed a **cheeky** remark, and decided there and then to hang Babette's wonder bra demonstratively over the radiator in the bathroom. Instead I told her that we'd already found the glove ages ago, and were just having a little chat. Anthony is sure to come down any minute. I pressed the left glove of my new pair of skiing gloves into his hand.

He thanked me **profusely**, even though my glove was green and wasn't even similar to his. "Thank you, thank you, thank you," he was pleased, spreading his fingers to give a salute of triumph, and disappeared again.

Perhaps Anthony was colour blind.

---

cheeky – vorlaut, frech; profusely – überschwänglich

I had to sit down for a moment.

Unfortunately, the dress was now so crumpled from being stuck up my sweatshirt that I had to iron it completely. After half an hour I had managed to get rid of all the **creases**, including those ones that I had ironed into the material by mistake. I regarded my work with satisfaction. Actually, Mum could be proud of how **neatly** I had lengthened and ironed the dress.

All that I now needed was a good hiding place. I looked around searchingly. It was no use. I had no choice but to take it to school with me and ask Tanja to take it home.

---

crease – Falte; neatly – sauber, ordentlich

Babette looked amused when I came home from school on Thursday.

"Henri, I must tell you something!"

"Yes?" I said indifferently, and went into the kitchen, piling my lunch on a plate. "What then?"

Babette sat down next to me. "No, don't worry, it's got nothing to do with the latest achievements in modern maths. This morning, just after you had left the house, someone rang up here." She looked at me searchingly and said in a deep voice: "Guess who's fallen in love with you?"

Tom?! Maybe Tom had rung up, and for some reason or other confessed to my sister that he had fallen in love with me? I couldn't believe it. I decided to start liking my sister again, and flung my arms around her neck.

"Ouch! Be careful with that fork. You're **stabbing** me," she protested.

"But I'm so happy," I said. "What did he say?"

---

to stab – erstechen

"What d'you mean, he? His mother rang up," said Babette, and looked rather astonished. "She thought I was Mum, and before I could tell her that I was your sister, she went on to say that it must have an end."

Now I didn't understand a single thing. Why should Tom's mother ... and where did she get our address from?

"Alright, to cut it short," Babette continued, **pinching** a piece of chicken from my plate, "she discovered that her Dietmar had written a love letter. And it is pretty obvious from this letter that her son has fallen **head over heels** in love with you. He's even written a poem, she told me. She doesn't think it will be possible for him to give extra tuition in his present state."

Dietmar!

Curly Dietmar had fallen in love with me, and he wrote poems. I couldn't help myself, I just had to laugh out loud. Anthony heard us, sat down with us and joined in the laughter even though he certainly didn't understand a word of our conversation.

After a while, Babette became serious again. "It's not right for us to make fun of Dietmar's feelings. We'll keep it a secret." She cleared her throat. "Of course, I could **no longer** tell Dr Caberg that I was

---

to pinch – stibitzen; head over heels – bis über beide Ohren; no longer – nicht mehr

not your mother. We agreed not to have any more extra lessons until Dietmar has calmed down again, and that Dad is to ring her up after the next maths test.

"That means that if the test **turns out well**, then I won't need any more extra tuition," I said with satisfaction. I was almost certain I would get as good grades as before. Caberg would certainly give me every possible mark, just to protect her Dietmar from me.

"And why doesn't she want Dietmar to fall in love with me?" I inquired. "Has she got something against me?"

Babette laughed. "Come on, just think about it: Caberg. It's got nothing to do with you; I'm sure she thinks you're quite nice. No, I think she is terribly old-fashioned, and doesn't think that you're supposed to fall in love until you've **come of age**. In her eyes, Dietmar is simply too young for it." Babette took me by the chin, and turned my head to look her straight in the face. "Were you thinking of anyone else just now, by any chance?"

"Uh, not really," I fibbed.

My sister regarded me, thoughtfully. "Yes, well, you are only fourteen," she said finally.

Babette thinks just like Caberg, I was surprised to note.

---

to turn out well – gut ausfallen; to come of age – volljährig werden

"When did you fall in love for the first time?" I asked curiously.

Babette shrugged her shoulders. "Don't know any more," she claimed. "I can't even remember what his name was."

I'll never forget Tom, I resolved. And when I'm eighty-five, I'll always remember that the love of my life was called Tom.

I'd arranged to go to Tanja's on Saturday afternoon so that we would have enough time to "**get dolled up**" for the fancy-dress ball, as Tanja kept saying.

"I don't know why you want to go to Tanja's first," Dad wondered. "It's only ten minutes from here to the sports hall."

I mumbled that we wanted to put on some make-up, and do our hair. And besides, Babette's room was so small that Tanja couldn't come to visit me there.

"Alright then! Babette will come and collect you in the car at ten o'clock," he said finally. "You'll be waiting at the entrance on time, do you understand?"

"By the way, Henriette, we've got something for you," shouted Mum, coming into the room with a plastic bag. "Just imagine, I nearly forgot." She pulled a red and white striped T-shirt, and a pair of navy-blue leggings out of the bag. "You said you really wanted a new fancy-dress costume."

---

to get dolled up – sich herausputzen, aufdonnern

I swallowed. "Thanks," I said in an undertone.

"What's wrong? Don't you like it?" inquired Mum. "Look here!" She handed me a bright yellow **rubber duck**. "It's a bit of a joke, isn't it? You really must take it with you."

I assured everyone that I was really looking forward to the evening dressed as a sailor with a bright-yellow rubber duck, but, I was sorry, I had to go to Tanja's now.

"Don't you want to try them on at least?" asked Mum disappointed, when I was standing in the hallway, looking for my anorak. "I'd love to see how the striped shirt suits you."

"No time. I'll miss the tram, otherwise," I said, and stuffed Mum's present carelessly into my bag. "But I'll go around as a sailor all day long tomorrow, if you want."

"Put some gloves on!" Dad shouted after me. "It's minus three degrees."

At Tanja's, you could already hear the typical carnival music on the stairs. Bright fairy lights were hanging on the front door, flashing on and off. Somebody had distributed a lot of confetti and paper streamers, and balloons were hanging from the ceiling. Tanja's mother, who opened the door to me, had three red hearts on her face, and lilac-coloured hair.

---

rubber duck – Gummiente

"Helau and Alaaf," she greeted me in true carnival fashion. "Tanja is already mad with excitement."

"Well? What d'you think?" asked my friend, and waved me into the living room. She twirled around in her gold-shimmering harem outfit. "What a pity I can't wear it in Berlin in the summer. Or maybe I could. What d'you reckon? Are you able to come now? Harry Willings will **faint outright** when he sees me like this."

"I'm not quite sure if that's the right thing for Berlin," I suggested carefully, but Tanja only laughed. And I could have also said: "I don't think that I'll be allowed to come with you to Berlin, either. You know my parents." But I didn't want to spoil the evening for Tanja, and so I decided to remain silent.

"Smile, please," she shouted, and pulled out a small instant camera.

"My mother has already taken four photos of me, and I'm going to send one of them to Harry. Come and help me!" She handed me four photographs that were almost identical. "Which one is the nicest?"

In all four photos, Tanja was laughing in her harem costume displaying her belly-button. I frowned. "I wouldn't take that one," I said at last. "You can see the **budgie** cage rather clearly, and that doesn't really go with your costume."

---

to faint outright – auf der Stelle in Ohnmacht fallen;
budgie – Wellensittich

Tanja nodded. "You're right. But I don't have to make a decision this evening. I should see to you first of all."

For at least an hour we stood in the bathroom, putting on make-up. Every now and again Tanja's mother came in, assessed our work, brought us freshly-baked **doughnuts**, and gave us some advice and tissues to wipe away the mistakes we made with the eyeliner and eyeshadow.

"Henri has made quite something of herself," remarked her mother in astonishment when I walked into the kitchen after a while, wearing the long black evening dress. "You look really grown up. Shall I have a look and see what your horoscope says for today?"

"Mine says that I should try to pay much more attention to the positive side of life, and not to make any comments that might hurt others," Tanja told me. "Alright, I'll do my best. Mum, let's hear what Henri's horoscope says."

Mrs Ostertag shook her head. "I don't want to spoil the mood. In the end she won't even dare to leave the house this evening."

"I had become curious. Go on, read it out, I don't mind," I said.

And Tanja added: "Henri doesn't believe in such rubbish, you see!"

"OK, you wanted it," murmured Mrs Ostertag,

---

doughnut – Berliner

and for a moment she gave me **the creeps**, despite her cheerful carnival costume. In a monotonous voice she read: "Mars and Saturn have a disturbing influence on your life. Great demands will be made of you now, which will require all your **commitment**. Tension and aggressions are now likely to erupt in a particularly violent manner, and ..."

"I think I must be going mad!" Simon, Tanja's elder brother was standing at the door and was laughing. "Heavens, Mum, don't **frighten the life out of** poor Henri. She's gone as white as a sheet under all that make-up." He gave me a friendly punch in the side to cheer me up. "Isn't that right, Henri?"

Tanja's mother nodded with guilt. Perhaps she had a guilty conscience, or she was sorry for me because of the lousy horoscope. At any rate, she lent me a lilac feather boa, and long golden clip-on earrings that I was not to lose under any circumstances.

"I had those from my ex-husband," she said. "But somehow you still cling to these things. When are you actually going?"

"I've got a suggestion to make," Simon intervened. "A **mutual** favour. I'll drive you there and drop you off fifty yards in front of the sports hall."

"Simon, you're a darling," Tanja delighted. "But what about the mutual bit?"

---

the creeps – das Gruseln; commitment – Einsatz;
to frighten the life out of sb – jmd. zu Tode erschrecken;
mutual – gegenseitig, auf Gegenseitigkeit

"You know the tall office block, right next to the hall? Well, I've got to deliver a parcel there this evening. But I can't find a place to park, far or wide, and the police are just waiting to **tow** somebody **away**. So my suggestion is this: I'll jump out of the car quickly, unlock the entrance door and you take up the parcel. It's only a few yards to the sports hall then."

"That's a good idea," said my friend. "If we went by tram, we'd have to walk ten minutes at least. But you've got to pick us again later. Agreed?"

Simon would probably have agreed to everything; he just wanted to be rid of his parcel that evening. He promised to pick us up again punctually at ten o'clock in the evening in front of the hall, and then to drive me home. I rang home and told the **answering machine** that Babette didn't have to come and pick me up. She probably wouldn't be very angry about it.

"So, ladies." Simon tore open the door of his small car, and we squeezed ourselves in. He handed his sister the parcel which we were to deposit in front of the office door on the seventh floor, and off we drove. A few streets before we reached the sports hall, there was already a **tailback** of cars.

"It's what I expected," Simon **swore** when we were only progressing at walking pace.

---

to tow away – abschleppen; answering machine – Anrufbeantworter; tailback – Stau; to swear – hier: fluchen

"We can get out and walk the rest of the way," I suggested.

Tanja's brother laughed briefly. "And I'm supposed to dissolve into thin air with the car, am I? Just look behind you. The road is blocked!"

"Besides, it's a one-way street," Tanja informed me. "Let Simon drive us right up to the door. Hey, Henri, shall we leave our jackets in the car? I think it looks stupid: a long, black evening dress, golden earrings and a blue anorak."

Actually I found it was really cold in the sleeveless dress, but I nodded. Anyway, Tanja would surely freeze a lot more in her short top.

"You two will make any sacrifice just for the sake of beauty." Simon shook his head with a complete lack of understanding. "Alright then, I don't mind. Leave the anoraks in the back!"

There was no vacant parking space in front of the office block because of the event taking place at the neighbouring sports hall. Even the fire entrance had been blocked.

Simon drove right to the edge of the **pavement** and jumped out of the car. "Come on, before the drivers behind me start protesting," he shouted, rushed up the few steps to the office block, and opened up the large glass door.

"Right, remember: seventh floor, solicitor's office Sänger, Sänger and Roth. You've only got to put the

---

pavement – Bürgersteig

parcel in front of the door. You can then **buzz off** and enjoy yourselves."

He wanted to say something else but all the other cars had started to beep their **horns** because his car was blocking half the street.

"Idiots," he yelled, "they're not moving up the front, either." He got back in, and also started to beep his horn.

"It feels strange," I said to Tanja as we stood in the block of offices, looking all around us.

She looked at me **inquiringly**.

"Well, yes," I explained, "in the daytime it's very busy here. And now everything is all so quiet and empty."

"Well, it is closing time. We're the only ones here who are still working. Come on, let's take the lift. Or do you feel like walking up seven flights of stairs?"

But the lift had stopped working. It was closing time after all, just as my friend had correctly recognized.

"We'll have to run up," I said. Perhaps this was the first of those great demands referred to in my horoscope.

Tanja seemed to be thinking along the same lines, because she finally said that a **heavy workload** had been forecast for her, but she would be able to cope with it easily.

---

to buzz off – abzischen; horn – Hupe; inquiringly – fragend; heavy workload – großes Arbeitspensum

"Right, let's play mountain climbers then," I said, and pointed towards the stairs.

Tanja nodded. Simon hadn't made a bad swap. I bet he was sitting comfortably in his room again by now, while we were still **struggling** away.

We rushed up the first two flights, and then got slower and slower. "We still need some energy for the rest of the evening," gasped Tanja at the fifth floor. "C'mon, let's have a little rest."

We walked over to the wide window at the front and glanced down at the street. The **traffic jam** had miraculously dispersed. One single car was driving past slowly – certainly in search of a free parking space.

"I'm going to tell Simon what we've done for him," said Tanja, when we at last stood in front of the door of Sänger, Sänger and Roth on the seventh floor, and placed the parcel on the doormat. "He forgot to mention that we had to perform **great athletic feats** first."

"At least we're warm now," I said.

But Tanja only raised her eyebrows. "There are other ways of doing that. We could have been enjoying ourselves for quite a while now at the fairy tale ball. It's quarter past eight."

We ran down the stairs, and Tanja tore open the door with a dramatic gesture. The two of us were

---

to struggle – sich abmühen; traffic jam – Verkehrschaos; great athletic feats – sportliche Höchstleistungen

standing at the door of the deserted office block and shouted out with joy. We were back in the best of moods again. The heavy entrance door locked quietly behind me.

I sensed the next moment that something was not right. Something prevented me from turning around. Tanja didn't seem to have noticed anything.

"Let's run over there, I'm getting cold," she suggested.

"I don't think I can," I said, and my voice trembled, not only from the cold. "Take a look at this!"

"**Stop messing**!" pleaded Tanja when she saw the awful situation we were in.

The back of Mum's beautiful evening dress which had taken me a lot of trouble to sew and iron, was now stuck in the door of the office block. Simon had the key, and Tanja was unsuccessfully tugging at my dress.

"Stop it," I shouted, "You'll ruin the dress. I've got to hang it back in my mother's wardrobe."

Tanja bit her bottom lip. "At any rate, we can tell everyone in school what an interesting evening we had." She **frantically** pressed all the bells, but it was useless. It was closing time, after all!

"Perhaps there's someone still working here somewhere," she mumbled several times, and then slapped the glass door with the palm of her hand.

---

stop messing! – mach keinen Quatsch!; frantically – hektisch

"Shit, shitty, shit, shit. We ought to knock the door down."

When she saw my horrified face she smiled. "No, don't worry, I'm not serious. I'd better run to the next telephone box and ring home. Simon will be here in twenty minutes at the latest, and will open the door. And I'll tell my mother right away that we won't be coming home until half-past ten." She waved to me and ran off.

I was standing alone at the door of the office block, and was freezing. Meanwhile it had started to snow slightly, and I wished that I had dressed up as an **arctic explorer**. I could hear the loud carnival music pounding out from the sports hall. A woman with an **Alsatian dog** was walking along the street. The dog discovered me, barked half-heartedly, and the woman called: "Sweetie, come here immediately, otherwise you won't get a dog biscuit." She pulled the reluctant dog away by the **collar**. I hope nobody from our class discovers me, I thought, and shivered a bit more. I would never get over the shame of it. I carefully tugged at my dress, but it was useless. I was stuck.

Tanja had been gone for ten minutes now, surely, or perhaps even longer. Why didn't she come back? Did she have any **change** with her or a telephone card? The most sensible thing, of course, would have

---

arctic explorer – Polarforscher; Alsatian dog – Schäferhund; collar – Halsband; change – hier: Kleingeld

been to run over to the sports hall, and to telephone from there. But, of course, Tanja did not have such logical thoughts. It's no wonder that she's a **dead loss** at maths, I thought **spitefully**.

I wound the feather boa more tightly around me, and stared into the clear night sky. I discovered Venus on the horizon, and if I moved my head a bit to the side I could see the **Plough**. At least that's what I guessed it was. Maybe I would see a shooting star, and then I could wish for something. Some time ago I would have wished for nothing other than to meet Tom, but I had become more **modest** in the meantime. All I wanted was to get away from this damn door without damaging Mum's dress.

Some distance away someone was running down the street. At last, it must be Simon. But where was Tanja? Never mind, I was just glad that he was going to set me free, at last.

"**About time, too**!" I called, and my voice echoed loudly in the clear winter night.

The **pedestrian** was approaching, and I quickly wished myself far away. It wasn't Simon.

"Hello, Henriettte," said Tom. "How are you?"

"Fine," I replied and tried to stop my teeth from chattering. Don't talk any rubbish now, whatever you do, I thought; just behave quite naturally and say

---

dead loss – Niete; spitefully – gehässig;
Plough – der Große Wagen; modest – bescheiden;
about time, too! – wird aber auch Zeit!; pedestrian – Fußgänger

something intelligent. "Isn't that a fantastic **starry sky**?"

Tom nodded. "Impressive. What are you doing here then?"

"I'm waiting for my friend Tanja," I replied, and wondered how long a human could survive outside at minus temperatures, just wearing a sleeveless evening dress with a lilac feather boa made of polyester. At least I had kept my nice warm **tights** on. You can't see them under the long dress, I had told Tanja when she had given me a horrified look.

"Do you still go to Dietmar's?" asked Tom after a while.

I nodded. I could hardly speak; I was frightened that my teeth would start chattering. If it had been the height of summer now, I could have spent hours with Tom here at the door. But love alone couldn't help me against this bitter cold, not even my love for Tom.

"And is Dietmar's extra tuition helping you at all?" asked Tom further.

I nodded again.

He looked at me rather strangely; he probably thought I was **disturbed**. He turned slightly, and I realized that he would go any minute. I could have cried, but I pulled myself together.

"And what are you doing this evening?" he asked.

---

starry sky – Sternenhimmel; tights – Strumpfhosen; disturbed – gestört

"Fairy tale ball," I managed to spit out, and then bit my teeth together again but they started to chatter.

"That's what I thought," said Tom, "I mean, the way you're **all dressed up**." He stared at a point right next to my ear and swallowed. "Would you like my jacket, perhaps?"

For a moment I had the impression that Tom was feeling just as unsure with me, as I was with him. I smiled and nodded.

He wrapped his thick jacket around my shoulders. I **snuggled** into it and took a deep breath. I certainly wouldn't freeze anymore.

"Someone stuck an invitation in our letter box, too," he said. "That was quite unexpected because we've only just moved. But the football club must have found out my new address."

"Oh yes," I said.

"You're interested in football, too, aren't you?"

"How do you know?" I asked in amazement.

Tom laughed. "Dietmar told me. He reckoned you were only interested in football."

"Not at all. I used to be interested in football. But now … well, people do change. But I'm surprised that Dietmar talks so much during extra tuition."

"Not during extra tuition. He's always very **formal** then," said Tom. "But Dietmar and I go to the same

---

all dressed up – elegant gekleidet; to snuggle – kuscheln; formal – korrekt

grammar school. That's why I have extra tuition with him. He sometimes talked about you during break."

What did he say then, I would have liked to ask, but I didn't dare, strangely enough. Who knows what Dietmar told all about me. I shivered and pulled the jacket closer around me.

Tom was silent for a moment. He then took a deep breath and mumbled: "Actually, we could go to the ball together. I mean, now that we've bumped into each other. Would you like to?"

Yes, Tom, I'd love to, and your question is the most fantastic thing that could have happened to me; that's what I would have liked to shout, but I remained silent. I **surreptitiously** pulled at my dress. Perhaps a miracle had happened in the meantime. But that only happens in fairy tales, as everyone knows. I couldn't move an inch from the damn door.

"Right, shall we go?" Tom asked again, and smiled at me sweetly.

If I said "no" now, I could forget him forever. Without saying a word I pointed behind me.

At first he looked a bit blank, and then he understood. "You're stuck!"

I noticed how he **stifled a laugh**.

"I'm waiting for my friend Tanja and her brother," I explained. "He's got a key for the door. You see, there's nobody here, apart from me. Tanja is looking for a telephone box to ring him up."

---

grammar school – Gymnasium; surreptitiously – unauffällig; to stifle a laugh – sich das Lachen verkneifen

"That can take a long time," reckoned Tom. "They're always either occupied, broken or you don't have any change with you. How much longer do you want to wait?"

"Actually, I don't want to wait any more at all. I want to get away from here as fast as possible, but …" I indicated behind me. "You can see, I can't."

"Perhaps I can help you." He pulled up his jumper and pointed to his T-shirt. "Seven in one stroke," was written across his **chest** in large print.

"I'm going as the **Brave Little Tailor**. You know that one, don't you?"

"Of course!" I replied. "Are you now going to magic the door away for me like in the fairy tales?"

"No. I'm just going to **follow my trade**," Tom explained, and showed me the large pair of scissors that he was wearing on his waistband, together with a tape measure and a fly swatter. "Or do you have any **objections**?"

I shook my head.

"The dress will be a complete mini dress from the back," Tom warned me.

Never mind. With a few snips, the scissors cut through the **material**. Then I was free.

---

chest – Brust; Brave Little Tailor – Tapferes Schneiderlein; to follow one's trade – seinem Beruf nachgehen; objection – Einwand; material – Stoff

In the hall

all hell had broken loose. We pushed our way through the crowds. We almost lost each other once, but Tom gave me an inquiring look, grabbed my hand, and didn't let it go again. Tom and me, me and Tom, Tom and me. I, too, held onto his hand tightly, and was dizzy with happiness.

I discovered Evelyn who had dressed up as a mermaid. Holding Tom's hand, I let myself **drift past** her. I saw how she was **eyeing** him **up**, throwing back her dyed-blond hair. But Tom didn't seem to notice her. Next to the stage I discovered Tanja, who kept looking around, searchingly.

"We've got to go over there," I yelled into Tom's ear, and pointed forwards.

There was a really good atmosphere in the hall, and it must have taken us five minutes to move the few yards to reach Tanja.

She looked rather relieved to see me. "Come up here," she shouted, "it's a bit quieter up here."

---

to drift past – vorbeitreiben; to eye up – prüfend betrachten

At that moment there was a lull in the music, and the president of the football club had hurried onto the platform to make a speech.

"I went to three telephone boxes. At the first one I noticed that my telephone card was empty. In the second one the receiver was lying on the floor. Only the third one was working properly."

"But then you forgot your own number," I joked. I was so happy.

Tanja looked at me suspiciously. "Don't talk rubbish! Of course I know my own number. But it was a waste of time. My mother said that Simon had left five minutes earlier. She didn't know where." Tanja took a deep breath. "I then ran back because I was worried whether you would survive in the cold. And you can imagine the terrible shock I got when I discovered that you weren't in front of the office block. But as I got nearer and saw the black material in the door, I realized that you had **set** yourself **free**." She twisted her mouth. "Why couldn't you have decided to do that a quarter of an hour earlier, it would have saved an awful lot of running around."

I was about to say something, but Tom tapped his chest. "Maybe you should **point out** to your friend that it was I who ..." He pulled the scissors from his trouser waistband, and snipped twice in the air.

Tanja stepped back. "Did you ...?"

---

to set free – befreien; to point out – hinweisen

Tom grinned at her. "Yes. Do you think I should have waited until Henriette turned into a snow queen?"

Tanja exclaimed in horror. "Turn around, Henri!" she shouted, and grabbed me by the shoulder. Then she tried to pull me away from Tom. "You've got to go home," she implored me. "You look absolutely ridiculous. He's cut the dress off right above your **bum**, and now everyone can see that you're wearing navy-blue woollen tights underneath."

I didn't want to argue with Tanja that evening. Besides, I was feeling rather warm in the meantime. "Alright, if that's what you think," I **submitted**, "I can take the tights off."

"And how are you going to explain the missing piece to your mother?" Tanja asked quickly, and for a moment I felt that she wanted to spoil my evening.

Maybe I ought to tell her that her golden eye-shadow had smudged and her mascara had run, I thought to myself, but then I felt sorry for her. She wasn't wearing glasses this evening but had new contact lenses instead and her eyes were red.

"I don't know how I'm going to explain it to my Mum, but I'll think of something," I replied. "Tanja, be so good as to keep our places for us. Tom and I are going to get drinks for the three of us."

Tanja wanted to say something, but Tom and I only waved to her as we disappeared in the crowd.

---

bum – Po; to submit – hier: nachgeben

"Is your friend annoyed now?" he asked.

"Tanja is not in the best of moods at the moment," I explained to him. "But she doesn't need a baby-sitter anymore."

We stood at the end of a never-ending queue at the juice bar. While the football president was making a speech, everyone suddenly seemed to have developed a thirst.

"It might take a while," Tom reckoned, but he didn't sound too unhappy about it.

As far as I was concerned, I could have stood there for days. Tom was telling me about the football club he used to play for, about his bad luck with injuries, and about his mad sports teacher who did survival training in the woods every summer. "He taught us a trick how to make **earthworms** edible," he laughed. "Shall I show you?"

"Yes," I nodded, "I've always wondered how you can eat earthworms at all."

We had already got our drinks a long time ago, and were just standing around until I saw Tanja come towards us. Of course, I felt guilty straight away.

"We **were** just **about to** come," I fibbed. "But it was so terribly busy."

Tom winked at me. Actually, I would much rather have spent the evening with him alone. But then

---

earthworm – Regenwurm; to be about to – im Begriff sein, etwas zu tun

again, I couldn't just leave Tanja standing there like that.

"Since when are you two back together?" she asked Tom.

He looked at her **puzzled**, and was about to say something when the music started again. I swore never to tell another lie in my life.

"Let's go to the dance floor," he suggested.

We pushed our way through the crowd in **single file**, with Tom holding my hand at the front, and Tanja trailing behind. In the crowd I thought I could see Daniel, Christiane and a few others from my class. I would like to have shouted to them: look here! That's Tom, my boyfriend. I thought he looked simply fantastic. And it was a brilliant idea of his to go to the ball as the Brave Little Tailor. Besides, that's what my surname meant, translated into English: Schneider – Tailor. So I decided to take that as a wink of fate.

I was happy and smiled at Tom who had turned round towards me.

Tanja brought me back down to earth with a huge bump. She tapped me on the shoulder, and pointed wordlessly to a table; a young woman wearing a red and white striped shirt had just stood up and was coming towards us. I dropped Tom's hand out of sheer fright. It was Babette.

"What are you doing here?" I asked flabbergasted.

---

puzzled – verständnislos, verwirrt; single file – Gänsemarsch

My sister shook her head, and brightly-coloured confetti fell from her hair. "You do ask some daft questions! I'm waiting here for **Father Christmas**, what d'you think?"

Tanja thought that was funny, and giggled in a low voice.

"By the way, Anthony and I aren't here on our own. Mum and Dad are here, too," said Babette.

"But you didn't want to ...." I said, completely bewildered.

"No, we didn't, actually," said Babette in a strange tone of voice, "in fact, our parents wanted to go to the tennis-club ball. Mum really wanted to wear her smart black evening dress." She gave me a piercing look. "She looked for the dress for a full two hours until it occurred to her that it had been hanging at **the cleaner's** for about three months. Well, Mum and Dad then decided that we should all come here because Mum didn't have anything else suitable to wear for the ball at the tennis club. Well, and that's how we came to be here." Anette and Robert waved over to me from the table, and Anthony raised his glass.

"Don't you want to come and sit with us for a bit?" asked Babette, acting innocently, and **made a show of** looking at my dress. "Mum and Dad have gone to the bar. They are bound to be pleased to see you."

Father Christmas – Weihnachtsmann;
the cleaner's – chemische Reinigung;
to make a show of sth – etwas sehr auffällig tun

I doubted it very much, especially as far as Mum was concerned. She would, of course, immediately recognize the dress that she had been looking for so desperately. She certainly wouldn't say anything in front of so many people, but the evening was **down the drain**. For me and Mum, especially when she sees the **back**, I thought.

I told Babette that I would rather stay on the dance floor with my friends for a bit.

But it was too late. Mum and Dad, who had only put on a bit of make-up, but had not dressed up, were coming back from the bar, and were about to sit down again. I saw how Anette pointed in my direction, and the pair of them turned around. They then came towards me. I took another good look at Tom for two seconds and then walked backwards towards the exit, my **knees** feeling very **weak** indeed.

I could hardly fight back the tears. Why did it have to happen now? I had been feeling so great just a minute ago. I hadn't felt so happy in ages. At the hall exit I turned around and fled home, running blindly through the clear starry night.

In the bathroom I tore off the **mutilated** dress, stuffed it in the laundry basket and filled the bath tub with hot water.

With tears in my eyes I went through it all over again in my head. If I'd gone to the ball as a sailor

---

down the drain – im Eimer; back – hier: Rückseite;
weak knees – weiche Knie; mutilated – verstümmelt

with a yellow rubber duck, I would still have seen Tom, and everything would have turned out much better. I had done everything wrong again. He must think I'm totally crazy. Almost every time I encountered Tom I had **cut a bad figure**. First of all at the till at the supermarket, then when I was delirious on the staircase at Caberg's, I bet I looked like death itself. Then when he returned my purse. I'd stammered stupidly then. And now this evening: well, that crowned it all. First of all I got stuck in the door, then I ran backwards out of the hall with my dress cut off revealing navy-blue woollen tights, as if I'd **taken leave of my senses** completely.

If only he could **get to know** me as I really am, for once, I thought sadly.

What is Tanja doing now, I wonder? She was probably talking to Tom. It would all come out now. That I'd pretended to be going out with him. That he doesn't play the violin, and that he's not Caberg's son. I felt how my face started to turn red. I would never be able to look Tom in the face again.

Somebody knocked quietly on the bathroom door. I started. Apart from me, there was nobody in the flat.

"Henriette, may I come in?" I heard Mum ask.

I said nothing. She gently opened the door and sat on the **edge** of the bath tub. Of course, she immedi-

---

to cut a bad figure – eine schlechte Figur machen;
to take leave of one's senses – den Verstand verlieren;
to get to know – erleben, kennen lernen; edge – Rand

ately discovered the evening dress in the laundry basket. She gave a slight sigh, and pulled it out.

"Oh, my goodness," she muttered, when she looked at the back a bit closer. "Someone cut that a bit **lopsided**. This dress is beyond repair." Resolutely she stuffed her dress back into the washing.

I could feel tears pricking my eyes again. I'm so sorry, Mum, I wanted to say, but I couldn't get a word out.

She looked at me, expectantly at first, and then pensively. She smiled a bit when she leaned over to stroke my hair like she used to, and said. "My little one." Perhaps because I looked so amazed she added: "it takes a lot more than **five foot six** to grow up."

I nodded. I was still nodding long after she had left the bathroom.

I lay in bed with a high temperature for two days, and slept nearly all the time. Several times I heard the telephone ring, and my parents or Babette saying that I couldn't talk on the phone yet as I was too weak. When I was awake for a short interval, I resolved to put everything right again. I would look for a job and buy Mum a much nicer evening dress. I would now talk to Anthony for a quarter of an hour every day, because it would please Dad if my English **improved**. And I wanted to be as good at

---

lopsided – schief; five foot six – 1,70 m;
to improve – verbessern

maths as I used to be. I also thought of Tanja, and resolved to be much nicer to her in future. It was only Tom I wouldn't allow myself to think about.

On the afternoon of the second day, someone kept ringing the doorbell like mad. My sister did say that I desperately needed peace, but Tanja would **not be turned away**. The first thing I saw was the huge box of chocolates that she handed to me.

"My mother says that something sweet is just the right thing for you now," she said as she sat down on the side of the bed. "That'll build you up. Heavens, you gave me a terrible shock when you suddenly turned as white as a sheet. You had gone before I really realized what was going on. **What a palaver**!"

"I'm sorry, Tanja," I said and really meant it.

She shook her head. "No, you don't have to be sorry. It can happen to anyone. I guess you just had some kind of blackout, and then …"

"No, Tanja," I interrupted her, "I'm sorry that I wasn't completely honest with you. The story about Tom was quite different, you see."

And then I told her the story. I told her everything: from the very first lesson of extra tuition with Dietmar Caberg, from the first encounter with Tom on the staircase, simply everything. Tanja didn't interrupt me even once. She had opened the box

---

not be turned away – nicht abzuwimmeln;
what a palaver! – was für ein Theater!

of chocolates, and was stuffing one after the other into her mouth – probably without even realizing it.

"So now you know everything," I said at last, and took the **last but one** chocolate.

She shook her head. "But why didn't you tell me the truth? After all, we are ..." She hesitated a moment, then smiled at me, but I saw how her eyes **were** suspiciously **bright**. "... we are friends, aren't we?"

I nodded and felt rather **rotten** at that moment. It's true, Tanja is a bit funny sometimes, and she can get on your nerves, but basically she is OK. You can rely on her.

I was going to tell her that, but she gave a small cry. "I bring you chocolates and then go and eat them all up myself. I don't believe it!" She looked at the clock. "I've got to go. The 'Heidhoferstraße' will be starting soon."

I wanted to say something nice to her before she went. "Tanja, about Berlin, perhaps it'll all work out if one of my sisters comes with us."

Tanja nodded. "Yes, let's wait and see," she said.

The next day I felt better again. I had moved to the couch in the living room, and was just about to fetch the remote control for the television when the tele-

---

last but one – vorletzte; to be bright – glänzen;
rotten – mies, gemein

phone rang. I waited for a moment first to see if Babette might pick up the receiver, but she didn't make a move. Perhaps she wasn't even there. On the seventh ring I went into the hallway and answered the phone.

Tom!

"We were talking **the other day** about earthworms and everything," he said. "You said you really wanted to know how …"

The telephone nearly **slipped** out of my hand. I walked back to the living room slowly and lay down on the couch again. I was suddenly feeling very weak again.

"I thought it was **daft** of me to start telling you about the earthworms, and then not bother to get in touch again," said Tom, stammering quite a lot.

"I think that's great of you," I said. "I really am interested."

While he was telling me about the different ways in which you can prepare earthworms, I caught myself drawing little hearts with a ballpoint pen on the front page of the television magazine. "And what else do you do?" he asked finally. "Your friend told me that you had already started feeling ill that evening. It was a pity that you disappeared so quickly."

I swallowed. "I've been causing quite a lot of trou-

---

the other day – neulich; to slip – gleiten, rutschen;
daft – blöd

ble lately," I said. For a moment we were both silent. He'll say that he's got to hang up in a minute, I thought. "Tom," I heard my voice say from a distance, "I think it would be nice if we could see each other again. I mean, only if you've got time, of course."

"Yes, that's what I think, too," said Tom and he sounded very pleased. "What would you think about us having extra tuition together with Dietmar? I don't know if I already told you, but my parents are living apart, and my father had a serious accident. He's in a wheelchair now, and is **taking legal action** against the **insurance company**. The solicitor does think that he'll win the case, but it'll take time. But I'm not asking you just because of the money. I just think it would be much nicer together with you."

"Good idea," I said, and my voice sounded hoarse. I hesitated a moment. "But I've got a much better one." My voice now sounded almost normal again. "D'you know, Tom, I am actually an ace at maths. Honestly, I don't want to show off or anything, but getting an A in maths comes as naturally to me as …" I couldn't think of any suitable **comparison**, and was silent for a moment.

"But then why did you have extra tuition with Dietmar?" Tom asked **in disbelief**. "Dr Caberg told my

---

to take legal action – einen Prozess führen;
insurance company – Versicherungsgesellschaft;
comparison – Vergleich; in disbelief – ungläubig

father that her son specialized in particularly difficult cases. He could even teach a donkey maths."

I laughed. "As for my extra tuition, well, that's a crazy story, but I can't tell you on the phone now. No, honestly, I can show you my old reports. I've always been brilliant at maths. And now, well, I feel that I'm **gradually** getting back to my top form." I took a deep breath. "And what do you think about having extra tuition with me? I mean, only if you can do without Dietmar Caberg, of course."

That evening, for the first time for days, I ate at the table with everybody else. Anette and Robert, who were talking about getting engaged again and wanted to look for a bigger flat, were also there, and together with Babette and Anthony, Mum, Dad and me, it was all a bit **cramped**.

"Great! Our little one is feeling better again," said Anette, **sternly** looking at Robert, who was putting a second layer of sausage onto his slice of bread.

"Little? You've got to be joking," Dad laughed. "Henri will **tower over** the whole lot of you."

"While we're on the subject, I'd like to say something," I said loudly, and everyone looked up as if I were about to make a speech. "I have decided to **grow up**. That includes getting some job experience. I'm now giving extra tuition in maths, and I've

---

gradually – allmählich; cramped – beengt; sternly – streng; to tower over – überragen; to grow up – erwachsen werden

already got my first pupil. He's coming next Monday."

"There you are. As I keep telling Anette, things will turn out alright in the end," laughed Robert, and put another slice of cheese on top of the sausage.

We all laughed, even Anthony, and I thought, one day Tom will be sitting here too, laughing together with us.

Von Zimmermann & Zimmermann bereits erschienen:
Mathe, Stress & Liebeskummer
Küsse, Krisen, große Ferien
Liebe, Chaos, Klassenfahrt
Schule, Frust & große Liebe
Küsse, Chaos, Feriencamp
Freche Mädchen – freche Ferien
Küsse, Flirt & Torschusspanik
Liebe, Gips & Gänseblümchen

Zimmermann, Irene
Maths, Stress and a Lovesick Heart
Aus dem Deutschen von Anne Dettmer
ISBN 3 522 17647 2

Reihengestaltung: Birgit Schössow
Einbandillustration: Birgit Schössow
Texttypografie: Marlis Killermann
Schrift: New Baskerville
Satz: KCS GmbH in Buchholz/Hamburg
Reproduktion: Medienfabrik, Möglingen
Druck und Bindung: Friedrich Pustet, Regensburg

Die deutsche Originalausgabe erschien
unter dem Titel *Mathe, Stress & Liebeskummer* bei Thienemann.

6 5 4 3 2* 04 05 06 07

Thienemann im Internet: www.thienemann.de

Freche Mädchen – freche Bücher!

Sabine Both

❐ Umzug nach Wolke Sieben – ISBN 3 522 17490 9
❐ Herzkribbeln im Gepäck – ISBN 3 522 17554 9
❐ Was reimt sich auf Liebe? – ISBN 3 522 17608 1

Brinx/Kömmerling

❐ Alles Machos – außer Tim! – ISBN 3 522 17563 8
❐ Ein Paul zum Küssen – ISBN 3 522 17613 8

Christamaria Fiedler

❐ Spaghetti criminale – ISBN 3 522 17323 6
❐ Risotto criminale – ISBN 3 522 16965 4
❐ Kürbis criminale – ISBN 3 522 17250 7
❐ Popcorn criminale – ISBN 3 522 17635 9

THIENEMANN

Sissi Flegel

❐ Lieben verboten – ISBN 3 522 17190 X
❐ Kanu, Küsse, Kanada – ISBN 3 522 17341 4
❐ Liebe, Mails & Jadeperlen – ISBN 3 522 17454 2
❐ Liebe, List & Andenzauber – ISBN 3 522 17525 5
❐ Liebe, Sand & Seidenschleier – ISBN 3 522 17609 X

Domenica Luciani

❐ Das Leben ist ein Video – ISBN 3 522 17241 8

Bianka Minte-König

❐ Generalprobe – ISBN 3 522 17125 X
❐ Theaterfieber – ISBN 3 522 17265 5
❐ Handy-Liebe – ISBN 3 522 17376 7
❐ Herzgeflimmer – ISBN 3 522 17338 4
❐ Hexentricks & Liebeszauber – ISBN 3 522 17420 8
❐ Liebesquiz & Pferdekuss – ISBN 3 522 17455 0
❐ Schulhof-Flirt & Laufstegträume – ISBN 3 522 17491 7
❐ Knutschverbot & Herzensdiebe – ISBN 3 522 17572 7
❐ Liebestrank & Schokokuss – ISBN 3 522 17616 2
❐ Superstars & Liebesstress – ISBN 3 522 17636 7